1 7 SEP 2011

Global Pop Culture

VOLARE

fashion
engineering
unit™

Das Auto, die Frau und was sie am liebsten trägt. Welches, wer

Maria

STYLING: GIANLUCA GROSSI. HAARE: PATRICK MELVILLE FÜR BRIAN BANTRY. MAKE-

und was? In bella Italia gibt es auf diese Fragen nur eine treffende Antwort

Ferrari Gucci Notta

Die schönsten Kurven von Maranello bis Palermo: Maria Grazia Cucinotta in einem Kleid von Anna Molinari vor einem 550 Maranello (1998)

F A S H I O N   E N G I N E E R I N G   U N I T ™

First published in the United States of America
in 1999 by
The Monacelli Press, Inc.
10 East 92nd Street
New York, New York 10128.

Library of Congress Catalog Card Number:
98-68731
ISBN 1-58093-039-5

Printed and bound in Italy

VOLARE
The Icon of Italy in Global Pop Culture

Mario Boselli
President

Raffaello Napoleone
General Manager and Managing Director

Lapo Cianchi
Director of Corporate Communications and
Special Projects

Giannino Malossi
Director of the Fashion Engineering Unit

Volare: The Icon of Italy in Global Pop Culture
is the title of a book and an exhibition that
comprise the second project of the FASHION
ENGINEERING UNIT, the multidisciplinary
research center exploring the culture of
fashion supported by Pitti Immagine.

Florence, Stazione Leopolda
January 14-February 7, 1999

Editor and Curator:
Giannino Malossi

Special Consultant for Scholarship:
Peppino Ortoleva, Cliomedia Officina

Special Publishing Consultant:
Antony Shugaar, Paraculture

Exhibition Design:
Achille Castiglioni
Gianfranco Cavaglià
Italo Lupi

Graphics:
Italo Lupi with Francesca Turchi

Special Collaborators:
Paola Antonelli
Franco La Cecla

Assistant to the Editor and Curator:
Antonella Mazza

Photo Editing:
Giannino Malossi

The Fashion Engineering Unit Research Team:
Carlo Antonelli
Andrea Balestri
Sybille Bollmann
Laird Borrelli
Nadine Frey
Thomas Hine
Mario Lupano
Giannino Malossi
Richard Martin
Peppino Ortoleva
Ted Polhemus
Marco Ricchetti
Antony Shugaar
Pierre Sorlin
Valerie Steele
Ugo Volli

Photography in New York City:
Leslie Fratkin

Editorial Coordinator, Italy:
Progetto Media, Milan

Editorial Coordinator, U.S.A.:
Antony Shugaar, Paraculture

Translations:
Guido Lagomarsino
Antony Shugaar

Production Editor:
Carla Mantero, Progetto Media

Image Research:
Laird Borrelli
Maria Teresa Di Marco
Antonella Mazza

Video Research:
Michela Moro
Camilla Pediconi

Exhibition Soundtrack:
Beatrice "Miss B" Venturini

Press Office:
Cristina Brigidini

Public Relations:
Sibilla della Gherardesca

Administrative Supervisor:
Sybille Bollmann

Exhibition Coordinator:
Anna Pazzagli

Video Production:
Ranuccio Sodi, Showbiz Srl

The Icon of Italy in Global Pop Culture

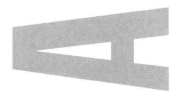

edited by:
Giannino Malossi

designed by:
Italo Lupi
with Francesca Turchi

THE MONACELLI PRESS

CONTENTS

What will become of "Made in Italy" in the era of the global economy that is upon us? Or, looking just a little closer to home, in the Europe of the Euro? I feel sure that this second project of the Fashion Engineering Unit—the interdisciplinary task force that is carrying out research into the culture of fashion, with the support of Pitti Immagine and with the notable collaboration of experts from universities and cultural institutions of all sorts, in both Europe and the United States—will provide some interesting new food for thought. The results will be of special interest to those who, for work or for study, have been pondering these questions seriously for some time. The fact that we are now examining the subject of the Italian icon (or as we put it in Italian, *lo specifico italiano*—that is, the relationship between the image of Italy and the products that, whether or not they were actually manufactured in Italy, are bound up with that image) is in and of itself an indication of a change in direction and of a feeling of uncertainty. "Made in Italy" grew and prospered throughout the 1950s and 1960s, and became the subject of international attention between the late 1970s and the early 1980s, when Italy woke up one day and discovered that it was now rich and famous, chiefly because of its fashion. From considerable thought and reflection concerning the underlying reasons for that enormous success, the reality of the Italian fashion system emerged: the completeness and unification of the entire integrated manufacturing sector, the organizational flexibility of the companies, the social and economic networks of communications and cooperation in the various industrial districts, the wealth of professional skills and abilities, the widespread entrepreneurial spirit, and the international mindset of the businessmen. Concepts such as Italian creativity, talent, and style find their roots right here. The total set of these unique characteristics continues to constitute the felicitous exception of Italian fashion in the international panorama today. These fundamental assets, however, are also the result of a spontaneous strategy that the most dynamic forces in Italy put together individually, in the face of the historic shortcomings of Italian society. Meanwhile, competition has become ever more aggressive, the markets have grown even more unpredictable, and customers are increasingly demanding. How will the inconstant, yet fundamental modernization still underway in Italy react to the present and future challenges? Will it succeed—after its successful encounter with several major structural issues—in facing the decisive themes of cultural identity, social cohesion, and the creation of a much envied civilization of lifestyle, a civilization that is, however, full of contradictions? That is why it is important to speak today about the image of Italy, to extract that image from its stereotypes, to constantly verify its connections and links with those fundamental elements, ensuring that all its components are active and looking toward the future, building it in such a way that it adopts the dreams, hopes, and wishes that are powerfully and widely felt, thereby allowing every individual to interpret those wishes, hopes, and dreams in his or her personal manner, claiming them as their own—in a world in which by now all places are present in each individual place, and each individual place is present everywhere. And we say this in the full awareness that the capacity to communicate meaning and identity is a powerful multiplier of the economic value that Italy continues to design and create, provided only that its industry—the fashion industry, and all other Italian industry—knows how to digest this resource and use it intelligently. This is the only way that we will be able to redefine "Made in Italy" in the twenty-first century. I am pleased and—why shouldn't I say it?—proud that once again it is Pitti Immagine, through this project of the Fashion Engineering Unit, that sets this matter forth as a problem for itself, and others, to consider. In so doing, we believe that we are carrying forward—in the area of fashion culture as well—the search for a better way.

Mario Boselli
President, Pitti Immagine

After sketching out, with *The Style Engine*, a first general mapping of the "intelligent forms of life on the planet fashion"—as one of the opening essays of that book and the large panel set at the entrance to the show ironically reminded us—Pitti Immagine and its flexible research structure, the Fashion Engineering Unit, are focusing their attention on that site par excellence of the system of forms in question: Italy. Imaginary forms or symbolic and exceedingly concrete forms of industry and advanced design are to be examined specifically and for the first time with a multidisciplinary approach. Pitti Immagine has previously explored a number of icons of Italy, but it has always done so in terms of partial views and interests: the icons of the early epic of "Made in Italy" in *The Sala Bianca: The Birth of Italian Fashion*, the title of a book and of an exhibition in Palazzo Strozzi in Florence in 1992 (the following year the exhibition traveled to the Louvre and, the year after that, to the Guggenheim Museum in New York); or that of *La Regola Estrosa*, a creative standard that Italian style has established over a century of men's elegance (here, again, the title of a book and of a 1993 exhibition); or else the icons of allure—largely "Made in Italy"—of *The Latin Lover*, a show and book dating from 1996. Never before has the image of Italy been observed from so many different points of view and from so far beyond the bounds of what is traditionally meant by the word "fashion," with the intention of recording and exploring the ability to produce added value through the icon of Italy in all the manufacturing industries producing goods and services with high aesthetic and creative contents, working within the complex system of "person-fashion-furnishings-home-food" and in the new global marketplace and culture. Even though it now lives as a citizen of the world, the "Icon of Italy" shows that it preserves solid ties with that very particular mix of real and imaginary qualities, material and immaterial, premodern and postmodern, which today can no longer be left to chance, but which must be the subject of conscious planning and design. Cultural research, once again, is in step with—and in a certain sense, leaving aside the issue of the independence of initiative, is an expression of—the work of marketing that we are currently undertaking through our trade fairs and the communications projects that normally accompany those fairs. For some time now, in fact, the shows of Pitti Immagine have been efforts to overcome, from within, the rigid barriers that separate the various sectors of fashion, and fashion as a whole from all the other references and actors of contemporary culture that run through it and them: this with a view to establishing contacts, opening unprecedented outlooks, finding new business opportunities for the players in our sectors, and even for our activity as fair operators. In a phrase, to give a voice and visibility to that system of "person-fashion-furnishings-home-food" in which Italy has thus far established its international leadership.

Raffaello Napoleone

CEO, Pitti Immagine

Volare

The Icon of Italy in Global Pop Culture

Giannino Malossi

Boeing 747 Alitalia sponsored by Bulgari, used on North Atlantic routes

This book is about Italy, not Italy as it is, but Italy as it is imagined to be. But what Italy is imagined to be, its "pop" icon, and not its actual identity, is what counts in the global culture that incorporates spectacle. From London to New York, Tokyo, and Moscow, the deployment of the icon of Italy produces phenomena that are at once visual and limited to the surface, and yet fully cultural and economic at the same time. An image, a container of conventional signs, engenders real consequences and effects, such as certain flows in the consumption of fashion. There is nothing new about this process: in the geography of the imagination, there is a great American dream, a French allure, there are all of the Victorian fantasies of the British Empire, the utopias of the socialist world, and many others. We have all learned, in other words, to live in the world of spectacle—reality experienced through the mediation of images. What is new, if anything, is the fact that such different dreams can coexist simultaneously,

intersecting without interfering with one another; one image no longer tends to eliminate the other.

Over the past few years something has happened, transforming, for example, the most elegant stretch of New York's Madison Avenue—known as "the Italian Mile"—into a larger version of Milan's Via Montenapoleone, but with the added feature of Italian flags fluttering over the facades of the boutiques of Armani, Ferrè, and Versace. Meanwhile, a major American developer is building a Venice in Las Vegas—Venezia, rising in the desert, like a dream caused by a case of indigestion. This is the latest ultimate design to exploit the mythology of the Italian landscape, taking no interest whatsoever in its actual geographic setting—whether it is among the aisles of the supermarkets in the chic well-to-do neighborhoods of all of Europe, where you can find whatever you need to make a fine *cena italiana* from spaghetti to tiramisu, or in the countless *bar all'italiana*, complete with chrome-plated espresso machines, *cornetti* on the counter, and the price list written in Italian (but in local currency), inevitably the most crowded places in the gentrified areas of the cities of the world. It makes no difference whether these are genuine old bars, where Italian immigrants once gathered—like the Bar Italia in London—or new theme bars, authentic in their fiction, cred-

ible but totally fake, where every detail derives from a coordinated overall image design. In short, what is it that makes today's Italy so different, so appealing? This is not an idle question, nor are these a meaningless set of coincidences: in a world in which communication is one of the most important economic resources available, visibility is usually an exceedingly expensive commodity, and image is a prized, strategic product. No country, however, is a corporation. Italy, by its tradition and political nature, is even less a corporation than other countries. There is no concerted plan for the creation of an Italian image—in fact, such a plan is inconceivable.

The visibility of the icon of Italy has never been a "powerful" visibility, except perhaps during the twenty years of Fascism, and even then with results that were not entirely persuasive. The money invested by Italian corporations in communicating a message is really not very much, in global terms, even if compared to the money spent on communication by just one large multinational corporation. And yet, assisted by the universal popularity of fashion—the only industrial sector in which Italy holds world leadership—Italian products are selling well in all of the markets where they are present. If it is the style that refers to specific cultural elements, that in the final analysis creates the popularity, success, and desirability of Italian products, the surfaces of those objects contain a description of the contents of the "Italian spectacle." The icon of Italy is the result of crossover exchange of specific elements of Italian culture and of the fantastic perception of Italian culture in the media-driven collective pop imagination, stocked higgledy-piggledy with clothing, art objects, automobiles, the neighborhood Italian restaurant, luxury furniture, articles in

magazines about world geography, memories of travel and tourism, old black-and-white movies, and lots of advertising. We have made use of these scattered fragments of the collective imagination to deconstruct the features of the icon of Italy, in an attempt to undertake a cultural analysis of the elements that comprise the geography of the desire for Italy, in which fashion, industrial design, food, and tourism are crucial landmarks, intertwining with other aspects of the identity of Italy in the context of culture and global mass communications.

This book is based on two hypotheses. The first is that Italy as it is imagined—its spectacular icon—has attained such a looming presence in the global mass culture that it can be reproduced mechanically (*pace* Walter Benjamin). In other words, there exists a cultural specificity of that

Preceding page:

The icon of Italy in the era of its technical reproducibility: the Bell Tower of Saint Mark's and the Doge's Palace of Venice in Disney World, Orlando, Florida

Photograph by Mahanam

(Grazia Neri)

Opposite:

Poster for the film L'Avventura, directed by Michelangelo Antonioni, 1959

(Farabolafoto)

The image of Italy has a mechanical heart. Ducati MH 900 E motorcycle, Prototype, 1998 Design by Pierre Terblanche, Ducati Design Center

UN FILM DI
MICHELANGELO
ANTONIONI
GABRIELE FERZETT
MONICA VITT
LEA MASSAR
RENZO RIC
DOMINIQUE BLANCHA
LELIO LUTTAZ
L'AVVENTURA
JAMES ADDAMS · DOROTHY DE POLIOLO · GIOVANNI PETRUCCI · ESMERALDA RUSP

Cinecittà, Rome

Photograph by Gianni Berengo Gardin

(Contrasto)

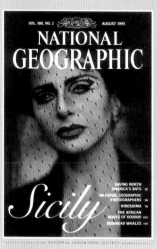

The actress Benedetta Buccellato

in a modern version of a Greek drama

performed in Sicily. Cover of National

Geographic, August 1995

Photograph by William Albert Allard

which is—or which is depicted as—Italian that extends well beyond the place of industrial manufacture ("Made in Italy"): Italian products are successful because they incorporate the depiction of the icon of Italy, that is, they contain an emotional quality, they are signs of a desire produced by the image of Italy, which is present in the minds of one and all. The second hypothesis is that the specific Italian identity, and the "rate of desire" that it prompts, is a resource for added value and for economic activity: another case in which an immaterial entity, cultural in nature, interferes with the cold material quality of economic data and industrial manufacturing.

Consequently, by working on the cultural identity of Italy, it is possible to design "Italian products" that best respond to the demand for "Italian style," making the best of the immaterial value contained therein. Recognition of the cultural quality underlying the success of Italian products entails, on the one hand, a redefinition of the mantra "Made in Italy"—a nineteenth-century definition that refers to a "law on marks of fabrication" put into effect in 1887 by the British Empire—which for too long amounted to a simplistic panegyric in favor of exportation; and, on the other hand, a deeply rooted and equally nineteenth-century idea that culture is a separate element, incompatible with economic reality. If the success of Italian fashion and design are crucial factors in the economy of the Bel Paese, the future of the Italian economy is bound up with the exceedingly slim thread of the capacity of Italian manufacturers to promote and metabolize contemporary culture in the terms and manners in which it is expressed, both at the highest levels and in the sphere of the ordinary and the everyday.

It is lucky for the Italian economy that it is expressed primarily in an array of "Italian" objects that contain symbolic qualities, but also technological and industrial qualities: what is that red Italian racing motorcycle doing parked in such an ostentatious manner in front of the famous contemporary art museum? It seems like a sculpture, and yet it holds numerous world championship titles. Why do the magazines that circulate among the neo-elites always devote so much space to new Italian furniture? Because they are the product of a culture of industrial design that dates back to the 1930s, which satisfies the needs for "cultured" display on the part of the well-to-do. Why are 80 percent of the fabrics used by designers around the world made in Italy? Because they are the finest fabrics, and they are always delivered on time. The challenge for the Italian industrial system is to reconcile not so much form and function, or production cost and retail price, but rather the cultural qualities, the signifiers, and the actual use of Italian products.

In turn, the icon of Italy influences the perception that the Italians have of themselves, in a series of mirror images and reflections that reveals the new mechanisms at work in the relations between media, marketplace, industry, and society—and, in the final analysis, the relationship between reality and imagination. This one aspect runs through all "national" mass cultures now dealing with the global flows of communications and capital; clearly, it is not limited to the Italian identity. In any case, one thing is certain: the icon of Italy has millions of fans around the world. And, as the philosopher of Graceland put it so well, millions of fans can't be wrong.

The New Hyperspace of Sociability: Italian Style ?

Saskia Sassen

Rigatone, container for
spaghetti, Alessi, 1998
Design by Stefano Giovannoni

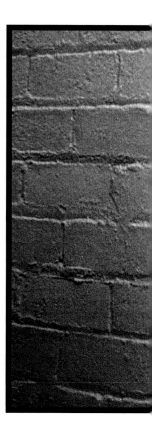

There is a kind of space many of us inhabit at least some of the time most days, whether we are at home or work, in New York or Milan, Sydney or São Paulo. Its topography is marked by a designer version of mostly familiar implements and activities, and the invention of a few new ones we did not know we could use, let alone need. Having a coffee or buying a pot is a transformed event in this space: stunning architecture, extraordinary varieties of coffee beans and kitchen tools described in complex detail, an ambiguity as to what it is that is actually being sold.

The fact that it deals with pots and pans does not preclude this space from being strategic. It is. Its economic and cultural influence vastly transcends its size and volume. It involves a minority of people, places and goods, but it has invaded the public imagination; an iconography of desire that spurs consumption of its own second-rate replicas and transforms the activity of consuming. Consuming becomes an act unto itself. The pot, either the designer or the downscale version, is bound to look different in the kitchens most people have than in the shop where it was bought. But that may not take away from the experience of shopping for that pot and spending time in that new hyperspace or its cheaper versions. Culturally, the idea of design and style has invaded just about all markets. In so doing, it has transformed shopping into a different type of activity, away from the instrumental and toward performance, a form of sociability.

This new hyperspace of sociability had to be produced. It is not just a given. There are the broader economic and technical conditions that make it possible, that can sustain its peculiar finances—hyperpricing, hyper-business costs, global span. And then there are, more

30

narrowly, the agents who produced the cultural iconography that is the oil that makes the machinery work, and work so well, around the world, and with global resonance: the latté bar in Bombay next to the Prada boutique made you feel just a bit more at home (and you may not have even noticed the shadow cast by the new office building of Deutsche Bank).

Key among the broader technical and economic conditions that make this new space of sociability possible is the new transnational world of work and the associated information technologies. The top-level management, servicing, and command functions of the new global economy are disproportionately concentrated in a worldwide cross-border network of global cities. The complexity of these functions has risen enormously with globalization and digitalization. The glamour and power and earnings of the professionals involved has risen equally as their work has become strategic for the new global economy. There is more internationalism and cosmopolitanism in their work and in their lifestyles.

The new transnational class of executives and professionals moves easily from one major city in the world to another, because it moves largely in this tight topography that contains familiar work and living environments no matter where they are in the world. It is not so much moving between countries as within a transnational, partly deterritorialized space.

Anonymous graffiti on a wall
in Little Collins Street, Melbourne,
Australia, 1996
Photograph by Giannino Malossi

Opposite:

Merdolino toilet brush,

Alessi, 1994

Design by Stefano Giovannoni

Pino kitchen funnel,

Alessi, 1998

Design by Stefano Giovannoni

and Miriam Mirri

The topography of their operations moves from digital space to actual space, in a strategic geography that implants itself in areas of major cities. But the growing digitalization of economic activities has not eliminated the need for major international business and financial centers and all the material resources they concentrate, from state-of-the-art telematics infrastructure to brain talent. In fact, there is no fully dematerialized firm or industry. Even the most advanced information industries, such as finance, are installed only partly in elec-

tronic space. And it is no different for industries that produce digital products, such as software.

It is perhaps one of the great ironies of our time that in an era of telecommunications and globalization place is central to the multiple circuits through which economic globalization is constituted. One strategic type of place for these developments is the city. As has been remarked over and over, there are massive trends toward the spatial dispersal of economic activities at the metropolitan, national, and global levels. But they are only half of what is happening. New forms of territorial centralization of top-level management and control operations have appeared. National and global markets as well as globally integrated operations require central places where the work of globalization gets done. Furthermore, information industries require a vast physical infrastructure containing strategic nodes with hyperconcentrations of facilities. Finally, even the most advanced information industries have a work process—that is, a complex of workers, machines, and buildings that are more place bound and are more diversified in their labor inputs than the imagery of information outputs suggests.

Centralized control and management over a geographically dispersed array of economic operations does not come about inevitably as part of a world system. It requires the production of a vast range of highly specialized services, telecommunications infrastructure, and industrial services. These are crucial for the valorization of what are today leading components of capital. One of the cen-

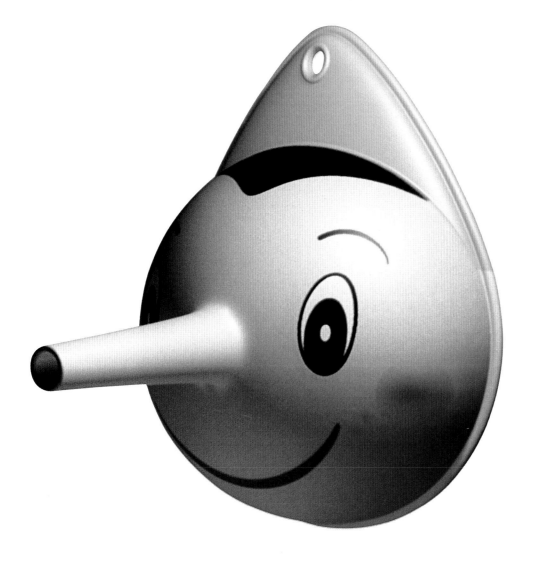

tral concerns in my work has been to look at cities as production sites for the leading service industries, and to recover the infrastructure of activities, firms, and jobs that is necessary to run the advanced corporate economy. The focus is on the practice of global control: the work of producing and reproducing the organization and management of both a global production system and a global marketplace for finance, under conditions of economic concentration.

Global cities are centers for the servicing and financing of international trade, investment, and headquarter operations. That is to say, the multiplicity of specialized activities present in global cities is crucial in the valorization, indeed overvalorization, of leading sectors of capital today. And in this sense they are strategic production sites for today's leading economic sectors.

The new transnational professional class is sufficiently large and influential to impose its work and lifestyles on the urban landscape of these cities. It is not like the old rich, who were and are a discrete presence in the urban landscape. The economic power, influence, and visibility of this class in combination with its size, which has grown rapidly with globalization and digitalization of leading economic sectors, is one of the key forces in the making of the new hyperspace for sociability.

But while the new transnational class of professionals and executives are the economic agents that sustain it, the space itself has spilled over from the narrower world of international business at its core. Generally, we are seeing the formation of highly internationalized

environments due to the presence of foreign firms and personnel, the formation of global markets in the arts, and the international circulation of high culture.

There is a whole range of new city users beyond the new international business class. They have made an often immense claim on the city and have reconstituted strategic spaces of the city in their image: there is a de facto claim to the city. They contribute to change the social morphology of the city and to constitute what Martinotti calls the metropolis of second generation, the city of late modernism.

Who are the agents that produce the cultural iconography that makes this new hyperspace cohere into a recognizable space across boundaries and nations? They are the designers and the cultural worlds they are embedded in. These worlds are particular, specific. They are not about some abstract notion of what is good design. They are worlds of culture that regularly explode the boundaries of what may have become established as good design. While they are often wild and eccentric it is not at all the case that anything that is wild and eccentric can become a pacesetter.

What is quite astounding is the extent to which Italy and, increasingly, a variety of representations of what might be Italian provide the concrete cultural contents for the new transnational iconography. This book is replete with specific illustrations of the Italianate taste of the new cultural iconography.

The new hyperspace has a topography that weaves in and out of digital space. When it hits the ground, it likes to do so in an explosion of concrete cultural spaces, overwhelmingly

Ermenegildo Zegna,
images from the advertising campaign
for the fall/winter 1998 collection
Photograph by Mikael Jansson
(Courtesy Zegna Spa)

marked by "Italianate" contents. The point at which this topography enters digital space, that intersection, is still often similarly marked: the cybercafé that serves latté is just one of these intersections. But what happens in that topography when it is in digital space? Does it finally surrender to the visual iconography of silicon valleys and alleys?

Europe by night, seen from space   (Archivio Infinito)

Faema espresso maker, 1998

Photograph by Leslie Fratkin

The Difficult Identity

Ugo Volli

Is there actually such a thing as an Italian identity? Despite the political disputes triggered in recent years by Italy's Lega Nord, it is difficult nowadays to say that there is not. Just what Italy is, what it means to be Italian, what the political and cultural boundaries of Italy are—these matters appear as clear to the Italians as they do to the non-Italians who study or watch Italy. There is a common language, spoken by most of the population; it is not difficult to identify the substance of a unified physical culture (food, drink, leisure activities, body of knowledge, shared attitudes). And, of course, there is an integrated political and economic system covering the Italian territory (a state, a flag, an army).

If we look more carefully, however, this identity—apparently so well established—is rather weak, because it is relatively recent. Roughly 150 years ago, as intelligent a political mind as Prince Metternich declared, in a widely quoted observation, that "Italy is merely a geographic expression," referring precisely to the lack of that historic and anthropological glue that constitutes national identity. In contrast, and not long thereafter, the Italian patriot Massimo d'Azeglio is said to have declared (though he probably never did): "Italy is made; now we must make the Italians." There is a vast literature concerning Italy's lack of unity, the Italians' scant sense of common cause, the differences dividing this people, which so greatly outweigh the similarities; this literature ranges from the laments of Italian poets to a prodigious quantity of articles, some of them quite recent.

In reality every identity, especially a national identity, is always the product of a historical and political design, never a simple given. For instance, the fact that nowadays there exists, peacefully, a Swiss and an Austrian identity—clearly separate from the German identity, aside from any obvious linguistic and cultural affinities—is an accepted historical fact, but it is the product of political and

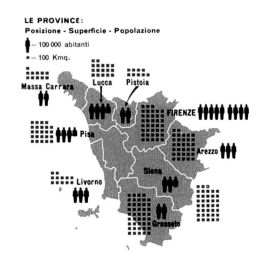

Tuscany, Atlante delle Regioni,
Istituto Geografico De Agostini,
Novara, 1956
Plate by Vsevolod Niculin

Sicily, Atlante delle Regioni,

Istituto Geografico De Agostini,

Novara, 1956

Plate by Vsevolod Niculin

cultural decisions, in short, of a historic process of the construction of identities. The same is true of the Scottish identity as distinct from the British identity, the Catalonian from the Spanish, and, of course, the Italian identity. A national identity is a semiotic device that serves to reinterpret in differential terms all of the contents of economic, political, and social life: this food, this song, this artwork, this physique or hair color, this phrase or form of language, this political structure, this form of organized crime—all are "typically Italian" (rather than French, German, etc.). As such, identity is a powerful determinant of forms of behavior, expectations, and interpretations. To an even greater

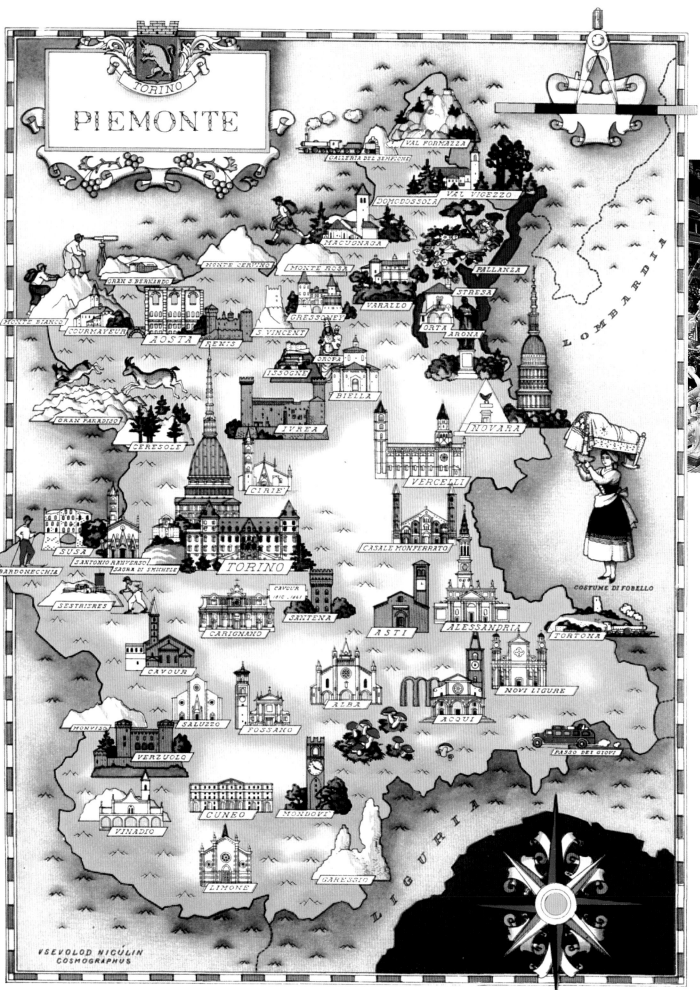

Souvenir stand

at the Trevi Fountain, Rome

Photograph by Thomas Ernsting

(Grazia Neri)

Piedmont, Atlante delle

Regioni, Istituto Geografico

De Agostini, Novara, 1956

Plate by Vsevolod Niculin

Traditional Sicilian decoration
on a Piaggio Ape motorcycle/pickup
truck, Catania 1998

Photograph by Melo Milella

degree, however, it is a product of those forms of behavior, a construction that is created in history, and in history it can decay.

In particular, this is true for the national aspect of identity, which is a form of organization that competes with other, vaster aspects of identity (European, Christian, Muslim, Western, Communist, and so on) and lower levels of identity (civic, regional, professional, etc.), over which national identity clearly triumphed during the century from the French Revolution to the Russian Revolution. Even now, Italian identity must compete with European and, especially, regional and civic identities.

The construction of an Italian identity is both an ancient and a recent event. In the *Divine Comedy*, Dante mentions Italy eleven times as a specific geographic entity, assigning it boundaries that are not that different from the actual borders of the present day; still, the *Divine Comedy* itself is explicitly the product of a cultural design undertaken by Dante, with the aim of constructing a cultural and linguistic identity. The political design that emerged—the construction of a unified Italy—took form only five and a half centuries later, and that was only 150 years ago. In the meanwhile, the construction of an Italian identity was the idea of an elite, chiefly an intellectual elite, that was cherished more by authors than by statesmen and was roundly ignored by most of the population.

The consequences of this centuries-long delay in the formation of an Italian state are not merely political in nature. To offer just one particularly significant example, the Italian language was—until the beginning of the twentieth century—a reality almost exclusively in literary terms, and was spoken only as the Tuscan dialect; it was not until the national census of 1961 that the majority of Italians actually spoke the national language instead of a local dialect, and these dialects are even today the everyday language of more than a third of all Italians. These dialects are not merely regional or class-based variants, devoid of prestige or structure or ancient heritage, as is the case with the dialects of French and English: Venetian, Sicilian, Neapolitan, Roman, and Milanese are solid and venerable languages, each possessed of a rich, ancient, and prestigious literature, and each is still widely used as a first language. The fact that Italian has always been an artificial construct as a literary language—to the point that it caused problems for even the most official of Italian authors, such as Alessandro Manzoni (who spoke either French or the Milanese dialect at home)—is something that still weighs on Italian literature, engendering that certain embarrassment, or reluctance, in producing credible everyday speech that is a typical failing of so many Italian authors; it is also the source of the incomprehensible juridical and bureaucratic gobbledygook found in so many Italian laws and regulations.

Another major consequence of the delay in the realization of the Italian state is the number of cities that were—for a greater or lesser stretch of time—capitals of their own large or small states, and that have maintained a memory of that condition, not merely in terms of a rich artistic heritage, but also in a more general refusal to feel loyalty and respect for a central state, seen in some sense as unjustly poaching on local liberties, and, therefore, as an outside oppressor. Civic identity (being Florentine or Sienese, Roman or Neapolitan), or at least regional identity (considering oneself Sicilian or Apulian, Piedmontese or Lombard), is generally much stronger than national identity. A civic or

regional identity is often considered a concrete factor, rich in consequences (in terms of food preferences, personal character, and so forth) as well as a value, and usually entails an attribution of unworthiness to other, rival identities (since I am Bolognese, I dislike the Modenese; as a Sienese, I detest the Florentines, and so on). The national identity is often seen as abstract and devoid of practical ramifications. This is the famous Italian *municipalismo*, which has often been viewed as an extension of family or clan loyalty, found to be quite common—especially in the south—by many sociological and anthropological studies.

The delay in the creation of an Italian identity —and the survival of other powerful identities that it has engendered—is not an entirely isolated case in the panorama of European nationalities: Germany underwent a similar historical process, and even greater fragmentations and uncertainties occurred in the case of the Balkan nations, leading to a fate of endemic civil wars. In comparison with what happened in Germany, it is evident that the idea of national unity was less powerful and attractive in Italy, and the anthropological differentiation of the Italian population was greater. It is clearly noteworthy, in any consideration of the relationship of the Italians with the unified state, that Italian political unity was achieved by an outside entity, devoid of historical and cultural prestige: Piedmont—governed by a dynasty of foreign origin, the house of Savoy. It should be further noted that the unity (really the conquest) of Italy was achieved very quickly, in the wake of skillful international political deal making, resulting in the ouster of legitimate monarchs who were, in some cases, also beloved. This contrasts sharply with what happened in Germany, where Prussia, an entirely

Germanic state, took over after centuries of political accretion of legitimacy. Moreover, in the aftermath of such a fragile conquest, the Italian government demanded the construction of a rigidly unitary state, enforcing the imposition of a bureaucracy suspicious of all forms of local self-government with harsh military repression, certainly a decisive aggravating factor. Finally, even in as brief a treatment as we are offering here, we cannot overlook the obstacle to national unity constituted by the presence in Italy of the Vatican (which acted from the beginning of Italy's unification as an opposition force, calling into question the legitimacy of the Italian state).

History, however, played a crucial role: linguists and anthropologists recognize in the distinctions between dialects and ways of life (for example, in the distinction between one cuisine based on butter and another based on oil, roughly divided by the line separating continental Italy to the north from peninsular Italy, along the Ligurian and the Tuscan Apennines) divisions that date back to the various settlements established even before the rule of the ancient Romans. Whether what happened is that the ethnic and linguistic substrates survived the blows and indignities of twenty centuries of invasions and migrations, or that those invasions and migrations simply followed the existing contours, the fact remains that the regional divisions that exist today— with different systems of speech and accent, but also with different styles of political and electoral behavior, and with the spread of such contrasting phenomena as cooperativism or organized crime—mirror extremely ancient boundaries. We might mention, for example, the well-known theory of Robert Putnam (*Making Democracy Work: Civic Traditions in Modern Italy*), who attributes the difference in attitudes toward the state among the citizens of southern and

Madonna on West Houston Street,

Manhattan, New York, 1998

Photograph by Leslie Fratkin

Preceding pages:

Sicily, postcard from the 1950s

(Civica Raccolta delle Stampe A. Bertarelli, Milan)

northern Italy to radically different conditions that existed at the end of the Middle Ages, with the feudal state of the Normans in the south and the flourishing of the civilization of the self-governing communes in Tuscany, Emilia, and Lombardy in the north. This division, however, which is certainly still alive, also corresponds to the borders that separated, centuries ago, the lines of Byzantine influence, or other lines dating a thousand years earlier that marked the boundaries of the Greek colonies on the peninsula. And we could go on, citing—for instance—the continuity of certain differences of electoral patterns with the old territory of the republic of Venice.

This is not to say that there is a destiny that links Magna Graecia to a flourishing local variety of organized crime, or that the settlement of the Cisalpine Gauls somehow marked out the geographic triangle that witnessed Italy's industrial development. Certainly, however, Italy's territory is marked by deep scars of history, and even when innovation occurs on that territory, it tends more often than not to follow those lines.

One example—modest but quite significant— can be found in the cuisine. Several of the icons of the Italian culinary tradition are actually quite recent. Pizza, as we know it today (ancient though its deepest roots may well be), is no more than a century old, as is indicated by the name of the basic pizza, the Margherita, named in honor of Queen Margherita, wife of Umberto I, just over a hundred years ago. Even spaghetti and macaroni with tomato sauce is not that much older: the cultivation of tomatoes in the south of Italy does not date much earlier than the nineteenth century. The same can be said of such northern dishes as polenta and various potato-based foods. Corn and potatoes did not become common until the eighteenth century.

Thus, Italy's culinary culture is fairly recent, and depends greatly upon the adoption of plants gradually introduced from the Americas, following the establishment of the great Atlantic trade routes. Even this new material culture did not spread uniformly over the Italian territory; it spread following the historical contours of territorial divisions.

Clearly, in the face of a situation of this nature, the first task facing all the rulers of Italy, beginning with Conte di Cavour (and of the intellectuals who placed themselves at the service of the new state), was to establish a mythology of unity, to trace all of the various and diverse histories—those of Palermo and Turin, Naples and Venice—back to a single event. In order to establish this horizontal unity of the Italian territory, it was necessary first and foremost to reinforce the vertical unity of Italy's history, referring all of the various local histories to the sole moment of unity preceding the establishment of the Italian national state: that is, the time of Roman rule. Therefore, it was necessary to overlook in general the conflicts—some of them exceedingly bloody—that pitted factions, states, townships, and families one against the other over the course of centuries, and thus to conceal the fact that the centuries-old changes that were fossilized in the physical structures of the cities (antiquity, the Middle Ages, the Renaissance, the baroque period, and so on) were, in fact, the product of nothing other than these very conflicts. Hence, there developed a specific concept of the monumental, resulting in astounding works and deeds, such as the gutting of the center of Rome by Fascist urbanists, demolishing the fabric of the city in order to highlight the landmarks of the classical age; there are other, less extreme instances, such as the effort to reconcile various periods within the urban structure, with the artificial introduction of landmarks that were

missing (for example, the reconstruction of medieval Bologna). This led, further, to the selection of a material and ideological culture of synthesis that survives today (the fusion of southern cooking with Tuscan cooking, the glorification of Neapolitan music, the myth in movies and literature of the *italiano brava gente*, literally meaning, "Italians, good-hearted people" and the title of a 1965 movie about World War II in Russia), resulting in such diverse phenomena as Venetian gondoliers singing the Neapolitan song "O Sole Mio" for tourists, and the neoclassic shrine to the unknown soldier in Rome.

The fact remains that this national identity is vague, unclear, and not much loved, that the periodical rallying around the flag for the national soccer team is given the lie, ultimately, by the constant practice of criticizing the national identity; that, in short, as Giacomo Leopardi wrote 150 years ago,

"the Italians have no mores, they have only customs; they have few customs and usages that can truly be called national, but those very few are followed chiefly out of habit." And yet—like certain souvenirs sold primarily to tourists, though scorned by their very manufacturers—that identity does quite well on the foreign market.

Opposite:
Urchins eating macaroni,
postcard from the turn of the twentieth century
(Civica Raccolta delle Stampe A. Bertarelli, Milan)

Pulcinella in Naples, postcard from the turn of the twentieth century
(Civica Raccolta delle Stampe A. Bertarelli, Milan)

Buying Italian: Fashions, Identities, Stereotypes

Peppino Ortoleva

This book and this research project are intended to capture something that may appear intuitive and yet at the same time is impalpable, or perhaps simply quite difficult to focus on clearly. Is there a link between the image of a country, that is between the ways in which the identity of that country is perceived abroad, and the ability of the country itself to create fashions, which is to say, to sell products linked to its image, and to establish its products over time as a standard, as a model that should inspire consumers? And how does this relationship function in the specific case of Italy?

What makes the nexus between the image of a country and its role in fashion so evanescent, so difficult to pin down, is certainly also the light, vague, and yet persistent nature of commonplaces. And images, icons, and stereotypes, are all, in fact, commonplaces. Each one of us forms an image of every country (including our own), made up of experiences of our own, experiences we have heard about, icons conveyed through advertising, books, food samples; we discover in time that, with small but not always marginal differences, these are shared images: commonplaces, as the name suggests. At times, it seems that a few newspaper stories, a particularly well-crafted advertisement, a shift in the tourist trade alone are enough to modify, in an amazingly short time, the images in circulation. And, at other times, we see just how difficult it is to shake preconceptions that have taken root over the course of decades or even centuries.

Exploring the universe of images and stereotypes, then, entails moving through a world that is at once fragile and durable, on crumbly terrain that is treacherously fraught with misunderstandings—misunderstandings between those who present an image and those to whom the image is presented, but also among the various versions and nuances of an apparently common image.

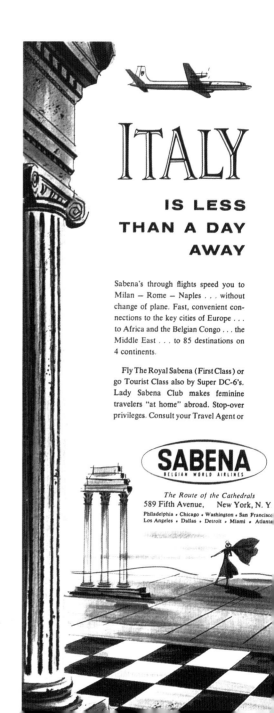

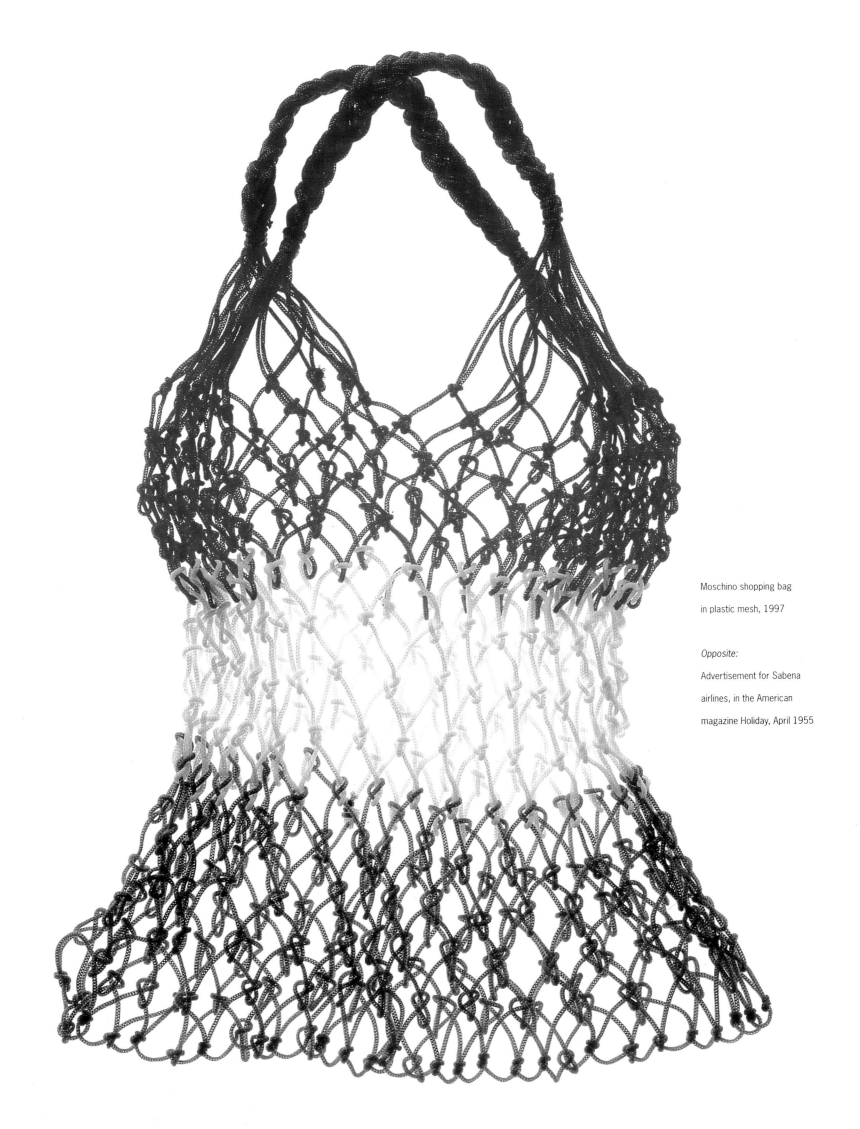

Moschino shopping bag
in plastic mesh, 1997

Opposite:
Advertisement for Sabena
airlines, in the American
magazine Holiday, April 1955

Key Words: Fashion and Identity

The very fact that we have drawn links between three of the terms that we have mentioned—identity, stereotype, and fashion—leads us to examine some of the most intricate and delicately contradictory points concerning self-perception in contemporary societies. And it is appropriate here to try to bring a little order to certain of these concepts, lest we engender further misunderstandings that tend to arise from the imprecise use of language. By identity, we mean something with which we feel we can identify, something in which we recognize ourselves, reaching beyond the various changes and shifts that we are continually experiencing, whether biological or social in origin. Over the last few decades, the concept of identity seems to have undergone—in various Western languages—a two-fold, contradictory twist. On the one hand, identity appears today as the crucial, central element of every social aggregate. Increasingly, we hear people using the term "national identity," for instance, instead of "homeland." This phrasing tends to emphasize the subjective adherence of individuals to the group to which they belong. The term *identity* tends to overlap with the term *culture*, taken as a heritage to be safeguarded and as a distinctive element separating one social group from another. Like culture, identity taken in this sense appears worthy of defense and preservation. When we speak of identity, then, we evoke—perhaps unintentionally—a need for stability, a need that seems to grow stronger in the presence of a great and growing rate of change and a continual variety of encounters and exchanges among diverse cultures.

On the other hand, especially beginning in the 1960s, a growing body of literature tends to underscore the variety of identities that each of us may don, along with the arbitrary nature of belonging to or having membership in a postmodern society. That variety extends over time, with the possibility of changing identity over the course of a lifetime, adapting to changes in ourselves and in our environ-

ment. But there is also variety within a single individual at any given moment. The elementary sociological truth, whereby each individual belongs at once to various groups, was overlooked in part (but only in part) over the course of a century in which center stage was held by the great ideological systems that focused on all-inclusive identities: from class to nation. Now that truth is taking back its rights, with interest (and with a vengeance): nowadays the term *identity* often evokes an image of uncertainty and instability. One symptom of this is the immense body of literature that flourishes around a psychic disturbance, itself quite rare, the so-called multiple-personality disorder, whereby within a single individual radically different identities may coexist without any apparent contact or dialogue among them. The broad and general interest in this disturbance is clearly a product not of its statistical mass, but of its symbolic importance. It appears as an emblematic and much amplified projection of a process that affects everyone—and all the more so because it is a pathology. Even for those who celebrate postmodernism, the proliferation and the uncertainty of identities evidently conceal something contradictory and unsettling.

When we link the word *identity* with the word *fashion*, it seems obvious that we are referring to this second definition of the concept of identity. This is what the anthropologist Ted Polhemus is referring to when he speaks of a supermarket of styles and, implicitly, of the images of self to which everyone constantly refers. Unstable and capricious by definition, fashion seems extremely reluctant to interact with long-term cultural heritages but perfectly willing to guide us, moment by moment, from one to another of the multiple personalities of the postmodern individual. Are we quite sure of this?

"Isetta, a revolutionary new car, not much bigger than an ice-cream wagon, opening in front like a litter, rear engine, a model so rare that crowds run after it: shown parked next to a remarkable apartment building with glass stairs, by architect Moretti." Vogue (U.S. edition), January 1955

"Scene: the ruins of Agrigento;
Subject: Greek design and style."
Fashion layout, in Sicily.
Photograph by Henry Clarke, from Vogue (U.S. edition), January 1955

Could it not be the case, instead, that fashion is one of the places in which these two meanings of identity meet and interact? A distinctive feature of contemporary society lies in the fact that its myths and beliefs do not take the perennially repetitive form of the always unchanging; rather, they take the apparently opposite form of an endless transition, with a few schematic and recurrent features. The great myths of the twentieth century—from the winning of the West to science-fiction accounts of time travel, from crime-fighting detectives to platoons of heroes alone in the face of a vastly more powerful enemy—do not take on (as do the classical myths) the form of a few narratives repeated endlessly, with variations of style and detail; rather they embody an endless array of narratives that are always different, yet reiterate a stable, and indestructible, outline.

The foundation myths of personal and group identities (just like the preconceptions about what is different from—or other than—ourselves) also often take shape not as a stable repetition of an unvarying icon but in an array of diverse images, with a substantially stable significance. This is the difference, for instance, between medieval and Renaissance iconography, which focuses on various scenes from the life of Christ (fixed, instant by instant, by canonic models), and the modern iconography of photography, which is made up of endlessly changing images, meant to be spontaneous, of an endless array of different persons, yet repetitious right down to the smallest details, where settings and models are concerned.

Compared with this iconography of the modern world—at once shifting and yet stable—fashion offers us something more: the possibility to experience and embody these images, literally donning them. We return often to the supermarket of identities, purchasing the same thing every time, with minor variations (which may seem enormous, but only through an optical distortion caused by extreme proximity), buying that with which we truly identify.

Icons of Otherness

The relationship between fashion stereotypes is also anything but simple or obvious. And it is no accident, because the very term *stereotype* has gone through a life cycle not unlike that of the concept of identity, being—after all—the mirror image of that concept. A stereotype is a preconception, in the literal meaning of the term, a depiction taken for granted, prior to any verification. It is expressed, however, not so much in the form of any direct value judgments but more in the form of an array of narratives and icons.

Too often, scholars and journalists tend to view icons and stereotypes as texts, as consistent, organic entities that require deciphering and interpretation. It is preferable instead to speak of a repertory, because it is often a heterogeneous array of things, whose strength lies not in its consistency but, if anything, in its ability to adapt to new circumstances. In order to be used in everyday life, in fact, a stereotype must have the conformation of a heritage upon which it is possible to draw at all times, but a flexible heritage, so that it is possible to find in it from time to time the elements that are most useful in illuminating concrete experiences, which are in turn fluid and changing. When fashion seizes on a stereotype and turns it into an object that can be acquired (an outfit that can be worn, a mask that can be exhibited), it is doing nothing more than reiterating the sense of both distance and recognition of which all stereotypes are made; fashion consumes that sense, certainly, but at the same time confirms it.

In its feverish thirst for change, fashion is, paradoxically, an element of stability in contempo-

Van Day Truex, director of the Parsons School of Design:

"In Milan Mr. Truex chose this innovative floor lamp, which he will use in his office at the Parsons School of Design. In Rome, he ordered a strictly conventional suit for himself, which he is wearing in the photograph; it is made of a light grey wool fabric, made to order by Gennaro. Also from Rome come his grey linen shirt, wool tie, and shoes, custom-made by Gatto"

Photograph by Coffin

Article from Vogue (U.S. edition), December 1949

Preceding page:

"The Best to Buy," a guide for tourists

to the specialties of the country,

and where to find them

Photograph by Arnold Newman,

from Holiday, April 1955

51

rary societies: also paradoxical inasmuch as it holds together apparently irreconcilable aspects.

The Power of Fashion and the Images of Italy

In this aspect, fashion's apparent frivolity is profoundly deceptive. On the contrary, perhaps we can say that for better or worse it is one of the prime reasons for the encounter and clash between cultures and stereotypes that mark contemporary society. What are the reasons for this surprising power of fashion, this function—apparently interstitial and yet essential—in the interplay of identity and belonging?

A first element explaining its power lies in its cyclical nature. If we look carefully at the repertory of images and clichés that make up every stereotype (of oneself and of others), we realize that, in general, there are unresolved and unresolvable contradictions. This is true of the intertwining of ineluctable technical efficiency and unbounded, almost anarchic, freedom (or "liberty in the stupid sense of the word," as Jean-Luc Godard once put it) that characterizes the prevailing image of the United States, both to the Americans and to the rest of the world. This is also true for the subject of this book—the icon of Italy around the world—which seems inevitably to present an unresolved overlap between a burning, exemplary image of modernization—made up of rational design and Armani suits—and a long-term image of tradition, featuring southern Italian cooking and film actresses from the 1950s. The power of the icon, its enormous allure, lies precisely in the coexistence of these opposing elements.

Fashion, in its capricious progress (in reality it is implacable), makes it possible to pass back and forth from one to another of these aspects, oscillating from an entirely Milanese Italy (food, clothing, design) to a strongly southern Italy and back again,

merging and extending these extreme opposites over time. The French sociologist Jean Gabriel de Tarde—one of the few sociologists to have truly grasped the dynamics of fashion—said that fashion connotes a society that is more bound up with its own time than with its own land (for tradition, as opposed to fashion, the reverse is true). This is a valuable point: the very DNA of fashion comprises a variable curiosity, fluctuating with time, about other lands and other cultures, with a commercial outlet in the consumption of stereotypes. Fashion orients the public, then, toward one country or another and (even more frequently) toward one aspect or another of a national image, inasmuch as it makes the public feel intimately contemporary; and this contemporary feeling is often surprising and paradoxical, because it can be based on ideas and styles found even in a distant era, though no less intimately perceived and felt for that reason.

Thus it contributes over time to the construction of a durable and flexible repertory, in which everything can be forgotten from one moment to the next but will later reappear. On the other hand, the widespread image of Italy is singularly well suited to a process of this sort. More than other countries, in fact, Italy presents a composite identity, comprising not only various regional identities but also various "golden ages" (ancient Rome, the low Middle Ages of Dante and Giotto, the Renaissance of the Quattrocento and Cinquecento, and the eighteenth-century Venice of Vivaldi, Canaletto, and Goldoni) and, above all, a variety of urban areas, each endowed with a unique importance in not only economic but also cultural and social terms. However great the allure of France as a nation, taken as a whole, the only French city that commands and controls fashion—for more than a century and a half now—is Paris. But in the case of Italy it is plain to see that, over the course of the various decades of the century that is now drawing to a close, the interest of the mass media and the commercial universe of fashion have shifted, variously, from Naples to Rome, and then to Milan, finally to return, perhaps with curiosity, to Naples.

These are different aspects of a single reality, but they are also different ways of conjugating tradition and modernity; and the powerful durability of the icon of Naples could not be explained without its absolute uniqueness in these terms. One of the leading and oldest people's cities in Europe, it has always been the capital of its own cultural industry, often provincial in terms of content, but supermodern in terms of organization, both ethnocentric and cosmopolitan.

This concentration of beauty and horror is bound up with apparently immutable traditions, and it is one of the few places in the world where the marketplace—as an essential instrument of social organization—rules absolutely. A city that is archaic in many ways, and yet remains one of the most authentic metropolises in Europe. For this reason, too, its role in cultural and consumer fashions has continued to flourish for more than a century, first attracting then repelling in an endless oscillation.

Cultural Exchanges

The importance of fashion in the interplay of identities and stereotypes, in the clashes and encounters among and between cultures, lies in another aspect as well. The circulation of fashion is bound up with commercial activities. Too often, in fact, we forget that in a market-driven society, one of the most important institutions controlling social relations, and therefore exchanges among different cultures, is the marketplace: there icons not only circulate, but they are purchased in the traditional manner in which anything is purchased in a society of this type. In the supermarket of identities, stereotypes circulate in the specific form of commercial exchange, which presupposes a variety of subjects and functions—somebody who will buy, and some-

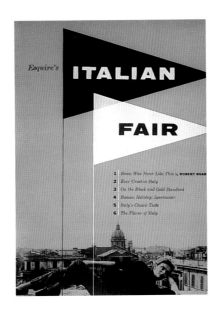

body else who will sell. The acts of buying and selling, especially when they involve products that contain meaning (such as clothing, but also food and music, and in turn the objects of modern technology and design), can be seen as a form—peculiar but essential—of dialogue, a dialogue in which each of the parties is putting in play not only their own identity but also an idea of the other's identity. On the one hand, when a person buys an outfit or a food that has connotations of belonging to another culture, that person agrees to adopt—to assume as their own—part of another's image. In exchange, they generally expect that certain values will be respected: among those expected values, there is often the strong presence of authenticity or genuineness, a true identity that obviates all masks and that is rooted in nature, tradition, or social spontaneity. On the other hand, anyone who sells a product with a cultural connotation—an identity-driven product—must clearly adapt that product to another culture (or at least adapt its presentation, if not its intrinsic nature); in exchange, however, that person will not only have the privilege of seeing others wear his or her own identity, but will see them begging, and paying, to do so.

The purchase and sale of identity-driven products involve a number of players: the design teams that create fashion products, import-export companies, store owners, and end consumers. This is a transaction—indeed, a network of large and small transactions—in which identity and stereotypes are continually renegotiated, with a growing sedimentation of continually renewed and readapted connotations. (A curious note: as I write, the social sciences seem to be literally obsessed with the metaphor of negotiation, and everything, from technological innovation to television production, is depicted as the result of processes—generally entirely imaginary—of long-distance wrangling between different social entities, which generally never come into any real contact. However, the genuine negotiations that take place between cultures and identities in boutique and department stores all over the world are almost never the subject of in-depth analysis.)

Milanese architect Ettore Sottsass,
from "Milan: A Capital in Search of a Country"
Photograph by Ugo Mulas for Vogue
(U.S. edition), November 1963

Giorgio Strehler, theater director,
from "Milan: A Capital in Search of a Country"
Photograph by Ugo Mulas for Vogue
(U.S. edition), November 1963

Opposite:
Illustration taken from the article "Renaissance in Italian Design," Vogue (U.S. edition), 1954, which in turn cites the Italian magazine Domus.

Buying Italian

In the final analysis, then, when the decision is made to purchase not only a product made in a certain country, but also a product that can be identified with a certain country, what is one actually buying? What does it mean to "buy Italian"? Perhaps if we try to answer this question—banal only in appearance—with some care, we can get a little closer to the subject of this book and this research project: why, and how, Italy creates fashion.

Buying Italian means, in the sketchiest of terms, at least four things, which can be distinguished in theoretical terms, though all four generally coexist in the single act of purchasing.

1. It certainly means buying a sense of belonging: those objects automatically refer, as if by metonymy, not only to a model of production but also to a set of national icons, the identities and stereotypes mentioned above.

2. It also means buying objects that were produced not only in a specific geographic area but in accordance with very specific manufacturing procedures and models. Italy creates fashion, if this is true, not only on the strength of a cultural image but also because of Italian traditions and forms of organization: the long-standing capacity to integrate industrial systems and innovative technologies with preservation of craft-based techniques and skills; the completeness—unrivaled anywhere on earth—of the production sector, which allows coexistence and cooperation, in part because of the geographic proximity of all the industrial players working together to create a fashion product; and even the tradition of fairs, which allows innovation—both product innovation and process innovation—to circulate with a fluidity not found elsewhere.

3. Buying Italian also means buying products that bear certain labels that have become established over the past thirty years: labels that epitomize the characteristics that we have just laid out, a manufacturing tradition and an aura that are both ineffable and essential, and yet hearken back to a style, to the distinctive qualities of a creative team, comparable in part to the tradition of a craft workshop, but in part also to more recent phenomena, no less mysterious, such as the professional groups of industrial designers or the programmers and inventors of software.

4. And last of all, something that should certainly not be overlooked, buying Italian also means fitting into a fashion, following the flow of a current that is already underway, a current that has been built up and consolidated over the course of decades, constructing well-established habits and well-known routes, a current that comprises movements of goods as well as of people. Would Italy be quite so fashionable if it were not one of the largest national tourist attractions in the world? As we follow this line of reasoning, we come to realize not only that an analysis of stereotypes and identities allows us to understand certain dynamics of fashion but also that the reverse is true. Understanding the dynamics of fashion can help us to better understand the ways in which stereotypes and preconceptions circulate, spread, and receive reinforcement in a mercantile society. These are two complementary points of view, which this book and this research project intend to reconcile, allowing them to interact one with the other. Likewise, they hope to establish a dialogue between the points of view of Italian scholars and businessmen, who are trying to understand from within the way in which the image of Italy is perceived from without and the points of view of others—Americans, French, British—who perceive and react to that image from the outside: a dialogue in which, as we said at the outset, misunderstandings are probably inevitable. But that is why the dialogue is particularly necessary.

In detail:

3. Pierluigi Nervi, ceiling with a floral image in reinforced concrete.
4. Franco Albini, base for a rotating sculpture that also rises and falls.
5. Fulget, floor with a mosaic of pebbles, for indoor or outdoor use (detail).
7. Piero Fornasetti, an enameled surrealistic screen with a slight trompe l'oeil.
8. Marcello Nizzoli, Olivetti typewriter presented as a sculpture in stamped aluminum.
9. Adalberto Libera, two varieties of marble used for the entrance to a building in the Roman exposition.
11. Achille and Pier Giacomo Castiglioni with Luigi Fratino, lighting for the "Permanente" of Milan; the circular apertures allow sunlight to pass through, alternating with large rectangles of artificial fluorescent light.
12. Piero Fornasetti, "who knows how to print everywhere," tablecloth and plates with newspaper print, centerpiece with roses in newsprint.
14. Ernesto Rogers, tent in violet and red cloth with a folding supporting structure made of metal tubing.
15. Angelo Mangiarotti, table that can be extended from four places (photograph, top), with leaves that can be folded individually, to allow seating of five, six, seven, or eight diners.
16. Roberto Mango, sunflower chair with wicker structure on an iron base.

An Imagined Italy

Ted Polhemus

A country is not a thing. It is a concept, a vision, a mythology. More precisely, it is always at least two mythologies: one internal, the other external. The former—Our Country—is what (hopefully) glues together what is in reality a myriad diversity of regions, ethnic and religious groups, lifestyles, and so forth into a shared concept of nationhood—a "We." The latter is a perception of a country from without, which categorizes and stereotypes its inhabitants into a particular "Them."

Shaped by political or military action, economic or technical development, and all forms of cultural output, this mythical "Them" then reverberates back to profoundly influence the economic and cultural vitality of a given country. In particular, export sales and tourism are highly dependent upon such externally imposed, mythological perceptions. To give a couple of simplistic examples: German car exports are aided by the external perception of Germany as a place of efficiency and technical competence, while German fashion designers and its tourist industry are hampered by their country's comparatively low ratings in hipness, chic sophistication, and fun; conversely, the perception of Ireland as a convivial, charming, and laid-back place helps sales of Guinness, the creation of Irish-style pubs throughout the world, and tourism, while at the same time denying the development of Irish technology and industry.

Obviously, one immediately appreciates that such mythological perceptions may have little if any basis in fact. The point, instead, is that however fictional, illogical, and even absurd they may be, such mythologies of nations and their inhabitants have very real and very significant practical repercussions. The other point to be made is that such mythologies of "Them" are often constantly changing. An enormous (and

Foreign tourists encounter Roman gladiators at the Colosseum, Rome, 1997

(Photograph by Ted Polhemus)

Opposite:

Gordon Scott in Il Gladiatore di Roma, directed by Mario Costa, 1962

(Farabolafoto)

enormously important) stock-market index of national values currently, for example, sees Cuba's Hip+Sexy+Fun rating going through the roof while "Cool Britannia" appears to be thawing rapidly. (And, who knows, maybe Berlin's Love Parade may in time raise Germany's rating for hipness and fun.) Year in and year out, however, the international perception of Italy as the world's centerpiece of chic, sexy, sophisticated style remains unassailable. We see this not only in the continuing success of Italian fashion (and other products that are valued for their design qualities) but also in the way "Italy" and "Italianness" are employed as positive terms to boost the sales of entirely non-Italian products. Thus a British ad for women's sanitary products is situated in Venice and the Swiss-based perfume company Aramis chooses to call one of its men's fragrances Tuscany (another, interestingly, being Havana).

The consistency with which the world has afforded Italy a positive and desirable mythological rating in the second half of the twentieth century makes it difficult for us to even imagine how it could be otherwise. Yet a consideration of Italian history brings us, at least initially, to a very different conclusion: that it is actually quite extraordinary that Italy acquired and held onto such a positive image.

First, there is the fact that not only did Italy lose World War II, it was (at least from an Allied perspective) on the wrong side. And, moral and political considerations aside, there are also aesthetic implications: Mussolini, the Fascists, and most of their stylistic creations (Milan's neoclassical train station, for example)

Rosignano Solvay, Pisa, 1995

Photograph by Massimo Vitali

were only slightly less offensive than the aesthetic legacy of the German Fascists (who, if nothing else, knew how to design an impressive leather jacket). So how did a country of unstylish losers come, within a very few years of defeat, to be seen as a nation of stylish winners worthy of international emulation? The answer, I suspect, lies at least partly in the very fact of Italy's defeat.

Forced to turn its back on its immediate past, Italy had no choice but to plunge headfirst into a free fall of modernity—in the process projecting an image of itself as more resolutely progressive and forward-looking than any other major European nation. Military defeat also had the effect of rendering Italy's success in other areas less threatening and more readily embraceable. In point of fact, it could be argued that the geographic region that today is called Italy has always benefited mythologically more from defeat than from victory, consistently spin-doctoring a successful and valuable image from a reality of decline and decay.

Certainly those wealthy young Englishmen (and other northern Europeans) who swarmed into Italy on the Grand Tour in the eighteenth century found particular aesthetic and romantic appeal in its ruins, symbolically underlining its former glory. Their copies of Edward Gibbon's *Decline and Fall of the Roman Empire* packed in their luggage, their own countries' industrialized economies thriving, these northern Europeans could savor the delights of a once great power now reduced to selling off its art on the cheap and readily prepared to convert itself into the world's first historical theme park: Fascinating Florence,

Duplè Aulla discotheque, 1997

Photograph by Massimo Vitali

Romantic Rome, Naughty Naples, and Virtual Venice (Venice being particularly interesting as the world's first city to make its economy almost completely dependent upon tourism—selling itself as a past-perfect time warp that, as rigorously as Disneyland would do in the twentieth century, obfuscated contemporary realities). A second factor, which at least at first glance would seem to have been an impediment to Italy's public-relations success, is the inherent contradictions in its national identity. For those on the Grand Tour in the eighteenth century (as for those more down-market tourists following in their footsteps in the nineteenth century), the principal, glaring contrariness was moral. Here was the very center of the Catholic church and, in art and architecture, the world's most celebrated visual embodiment of Christianity. But here, too, were those sexually explicit murals in Pompeii (which the guidebooks popularized with their prudish warnings); the free-for-all ribaldry of the carnivals of Venice, Rome, and Naples; a warm, all-pervasive sensuality that was shocking (and enticing) to northern, Protestant sensibilities; and the "dusky," even "primitive" beauty of the native women who, as the guidebooks helpfully pointed out, were willing to pose as artist's models for extremely reasonable fees.

But, as with Amsterdam today (whose dualistic mythology offers the visitor the choice between respectable art and puritan cleanliness on the one hand and easily accessible prostitution and drugs on the other hand), the conflicting imagery of that part of the world that would become Italy no doubt aided rather than undermined its appeal.

Concealed behind the respectable and praiseworthy motivation of cultural and religious enhancement, those young men on the Grand Tour could, in reality, partake of a rite of passage in all senses of the term. Taking their cue from Byron and Shelley, who sought out (and presumably found) a Mediterranean antidote to northern, Protestant prudishness, the young aristocrats and budding bourgeoisie on the Grand Tour could sow their wild oats under the guise of spiritual and educational enlightenment before settling down to respectable family life in their own countries. Ostensibly seen as a religious-cultural pilgrimage, the Grand Tour could safely provide that hedonistic release that Ibiza, Thailand, and Goa offer today.

In the twentieth century, Italy has continued to find success in its simultaneous offer of both sides of the moral coin, with the Vatican, glorious cathedrals, and a surfeit of religious art perfectly balancing the more earthy delights of Gina Lollobrigida's cleavage, nightclubs renowned for their excess, highly visible and barely dressed prostitutes, sexually titillating television, and the sexual nonchalance of *La Dolce Vita*. (Let me point out, by the way, that Fellini's cinematic vision was actually, in its terrible bleakness, as moralistic as Dante's vision of hell.) Just as this moral dualism had been of practical benefit to those on the Grand Tour in the eighteenth and nineteenth centuries, it offered twentieth-century cinema the opportunity to mount its own grand tour of pre-Italian history. Unwilling or unable to follow the lead of Fellini and others in depicting the moral license of contemporary

1950s Italy, Hollywood symbolically substituted ancient Rome instead.

Exploiting Rome's position as the geographic center of institutionalized Christianity, *Ben Hur*, *Quo Vadis*, *The Robe*, *The Sign of the Cross*, *Spartacus*, and a host of other films were able to bring to the wide screen epic depictions of juicy, salacious, Roman-Italian debauchery, while the presence of a stoical Christian message (and the safety of an ancient historical setting) got things past the censors: the orgy and bathing scenes, the sexy outfits, and the dancing girls sold the cinema seats.

It cannot be pure chance that Hollywood's fascination with ancient Rome blossomed at precisely the same historical moment—the 1950s—that contemporary Italy acquired its positive, desirable, and sexy twentieth-century mythological identity. In turn, the enormous, worldwide popularity of Hollywood's depictions of ancient Rome further reinforced contemporary Italy's own dualistic image of moral license juxtaposed with moral rectitude. For in so deftly shifting at the last possible moment from pagan depravity to the rock of Christian virtue, ancient Rome bequeathed a formidable public-relations legacy to its descendants—one that seamlessly welded together the temptations of the flesh with the salvation of the spirit. The Hollywood epics of the 1950s and early 1960s (like Gibbon's *Decline and Fall of the Roman Empire* in another era) served to download Rome's moral contrariness into the mythology of contemporary Italy.

In the second half of the twentieth century Italy overcame and then turned to its advantage another inherent contradiction

"Small World": Pisa, Italy

Photograph by Martin Parr

(Contrasto)

New model of Innocenti scooter,
the Lui, 1967
(photograph by Edoardo Mari,
taken from the book,
Tra sogno e bisogno)

in its mythology. Having eradicated its immediate past, postwar Italy could allow its antiquity and its sense of tradition to rub up directly against its modernity and its passionate embrace of the transitory and progressive—a collision of worldviews and styles succinctly visualized in the closing scene of Fellini's *Roma*, where sleek, black, futuristic barbarians on motorcycles roar past Rome's most ancient monuments (or, indeed, even in *Roman Holiday*, when Gregory Peck and Audrey Hepburn traverse a similar route on a shiny Vespa). Secure in its impeccable, classical credentials, Italy in the second half of the twentieth century could project a go-for-it futurism that rivaled even that of America (which, believing itself to have no past whatsoever, could only project itself into the future). The other interesting comparison is with Great Britain, where victory in war (but at a terrible economic cost) made it difficult for the present to free itself from its Churchillian and Victorian, class-based, stiff-upper-lip past. A new generation of working-class and lower-middle-class British youth, however, refused to accept this mire of history. Looking to America for its sanctioning of the newly minted concept of the teenager, the British teddy boys in their Edwardian-style "drapes" sought to storm the citadels of the upper-class elite. But aside from triggering an all-out moral panic, the teddy boys never actually threatened the status quo.

It was left to another, slightly later British youth group, the modernists or mods, to accomplish this. Rather than just looking to America and into Britain's own past for inspiration, the mods did something very un-British: they opened their eyes to what was going on on the Continent—in particular, to the modern, progressive futurism exhibited in the new Italy. In their "Roman"-cut (short and trim) suits, they sat in coffeehouses drinking cappuccino, radiant in the light reflected from the rounded chrome of a Gaggia, or they rode Italian Vespas to the seaside to do battle with the Neanderthal rockers who, like the teddy boys before them, hadn't learned to do the Continental. Taking their lead from Italy, it was these mods who first demonstrated that Britain, too, could pull off the blatant juxtaposition of tradition and modernity (so well visualized in *The Avengers*'s interplay of Steed's bowler hat and umbrella with Mrs. Peel's futuristic cat suits). So successful was this British juxtaposition of the very old and the very new that by the mid-1960s Italy's role in projecting a brave new world seemed to have been overshadowed. But as in World War II, victory in the pop-culture war would be Britain's undoing. The initial stylistic restraint of the mods giving way to the excesses of the psychedelics and Swinging London, and then, in the 1970s, the exciting but extremist experimentation of glam and punk pushed Britain into a trajectory that (however interesting) would limit its capacity to serve as a mainstream, international model of how aggressive modernity could be framed and balanced by solid traditionalism.

Waiting patiently in the wings, its own balancing act of juggling the old with the new even further perfected, Italy re-emerged into the world spotlight in the 1980s. Only now its

juxtapositions—of the classical and the progressive, of constraint and excess, of good taste and vulgarity, of the classy and the popular, of the good and the bad—would be rechristened postmodernism. A conversion almost as clever as ancient Rome's repackaging itself as the seat of Christianity, Italy's leap from being the definitive model of modernism into being the definitive model of postmodernism, at a stroke, made a virtue of its contrariness, its confusion, and its fragmentation. Suddenly, that gap between Catholicism and stripping housewives, between classicism and futurism, between the good taste of Armani and the vulgar excess of Versace, between the aristocrat's truffles and the poor man's pizza, between Milan's and Rome's contrasting lifestyles, between minimalism and cacophony, between the left and the right, between a young Italian male's respectable demeanor at dinner with his parents and that same individual's outlandish behavior at a nightclub, between the Madonna and the whores of Rimini... suddenly all this no-man's-land of all of Italy's previously inexplicable in-betweens became the solid landfill of its postmodern development. Because Italy has never resolved itself—never sorted itself out, never found a synthesis between thesis and antithesis, never got its act together—it became the perfect model for the fragmented confusion that lies at the heart of and defines postmodernism.

The most clever of all chameleons—just like Rome before it—Italy shifts itself into a vision of all our (divergent and antithetical) tomorrows. A skilled whore, it accommodates

Advertisements for the launch of

the Italian version of Roman Holiday

(Vacanze Romane), 1953

(Fondazione Cineteca Italiana)

itself to every client's fantasy—instantly becoming the nouveau riche glamour queen, the chic aristocrat, the innocent schoolgirl, the primitive savage, the refined intellectual, the mothering Madonna, the stern mistress, the wide-eyed hippie, the scuzzy punk, the naughty nurse, the efficient secretary, the glittering transvestite, the transsexual of indeterminate gender. Multifaceted, accommodating, flexible, Italy has become all things to all people.

While Hollywood projects one dream—the American dream—Italy (a giant, whirling disco ball of mirrors) reflects back any dream the world can conjure up. And every frock, fridge, Fiat, or pack of fettuccine it sells the world is a little, tangible piece—a souvenir—of this fantasy, not of Italy (which, as is appropriate to a definitively postmodern country, doesn't actually exist), but of whatever dreams of Italy the world has projected onto this chimerical facade. Man Ray once wrote, "Reality is fabricated out of desire." Italy is nothing more and nothing less than that fabrication of all the world's desires. As Venice has done for several hundred years, Italy now exists only as other people's dreams. But this is not a criticism—only a commentary on Italy's second renaissance.

The Italian Way to Modernity

Carlo Antonelli Peppino Ortoleva

Fashion is the most salient symbol of that feverish, tireless, and ultimately aimless impulse that—as Alexis de Tocqueville had already noticed as early as 1840—distinguishes present-day democratic societies. In the final analysis, if fashion tells us anything at all, its message is that everything changes continually. This is its profound link with societies that, for the first time in history, define themselves as modern—defining their identity, in other words, not in accordance with some past time, but with the specific contingent present that they occupy.

Fashion, the Present, the Past

The dynamic of fashion, then, acts as a great and common social calendar marking the passage of time, and especially teaching us to distinguish right down to the smallest nuances that which is "of today," or better yet, of the near, almost-present future from that which is passé, even only slightly out-of-date: "as old as yesterday's newspaper," to borrow a phrase from the bebop culture so dear to Marshall McLuhan.

If, however, we consider fashion as a sign of modern times, we see only one aspect of the problem. There is another aspect, at first blush quite the opposite, but in reality complementary. Fashion, in fact, metabolizes the continual repechage, or revival, of elements borrowed from various ages of the past. This observation is, in and of itself, quite obvious: from Vivienne Westwood's bodice to the revival of the 1960s undertaken in the early 1980s, the cyclical dynamic of fashion is apparent. Less evident is the fact that often, precisely in the most fertile moments of the modernizing process, what is revived consists of deliberately archaic features, outrageously premodern, from different societies. The best-known example—though still quite surprising, if we consider it carefully—is the reappearance of the lace and cut of the suits of the Edwardian age in the clothing of the English teddy boys, the substrate that gave rise to rock culture. Equally significant are the many revivals of various localisms—of clothing and speech—that have accompanied, in many Western nations, the extreme modernity of the last two decades.

In other sectors highly symbolic of social life, something similar happened as well. Thus, in all nations, the repertory of cuisine, though it generally developed and was codified during the century of industrialization (the century that also produced cookbooks, which still serve as the basic point of reference; the century in which a "national" cuisine developed in various countries), never avowedly hearkens back to customs and traditions typical of industrial society; instead, the preference is to claim premodern roots, whether aristocratic or peasant, setting forth traditions that in some cases have been invented out of whole cloth. And with nouvelle

cuisine we came to postmodernism, skipping modernity entirely.

Compared to cooking, fashion has been more ecumenical. It does not reject objects and accessories that are recognizably part of the industrial age, but it loves to integrate them with objects that are clearly premodern, and if possible with glimpses and allusions to an imaginary future: dating back to the 1930s at least, but perhaps to the beginning of the twentieth century, science fiction has been conditioning the way we dress (as well as the way we furnish and build our houses, as William Gibson pointed out) in Western society. In short, fashion seems to flirt systematically with the variety of historic ages and with their combination, in short, with what the German philosopher Ernst Bloch called the "synchronism of the nonsynchronic."

Not only does fashion offer up a repertoire of objects and idiosyncrasies from various eras, but it plays at once with modernity—as banner and language—and the opposite of modernity, or better still, the various opposites of modernity, be they archaic or postmodern. And this is all the more evident today at a time during which the modern era appears outmoded, and yet may have reached its true apex.

If it is true that the modern era explored in a radically new way the then current concepts of space and time to the point that everything that was solid melted into air, then this nonsynchronicity will appear to us as rich in the detritus of that dematerialization, of slips and references and post-everything winks of the eye, die-hard survivals as well as ironic revivals. The fashion of the last few decades certainly belongs to a contingent time, but not to the present as it is traditionally

"The New Fiat 500," 1957, advertising photograph

(Touring Club Italiano—Archivi Alinari)

Lamborghini Marzal, 1969   (Farabolafoto)

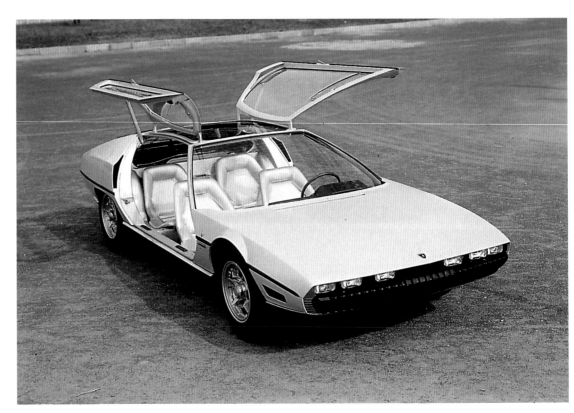

understood: rather, it belongs to a time and space where "current" means "everything," where the instant comprehends anytime and anyplace, where this instant that can be extended to infinity, that is always individual and personal, becomes the only possible society.

Modernity Ahead of Its Time
and a Failure to Modernize in the Image of Italy

If this is true, perhaps one of the secrets of the international success of Italian fashion is this peculiar relationship of the country with modernity. For many centuries—at the very least, from the fourteenth to the seventeenth centuries—Italy was in the vanguard of modernity. Long before other countries, it inaugurated models of protoindustrial production, combining the practice of craftsmanship with the early use of machinery—sometimes hand driven and sometimes waterpowered—in the Florentine manufactures of linen, or in the Lombard and Ligurian manufactures of silk. It is still possible in some regions (Tuscany, Lombardy, Venetia, Marches) to trace an unbroken line of continuity in manufacturing traditions, especially in sectors tied to the fashion industry (ranging from textiles to leather), often carelessly described as craft traditions, while their true value lies in the intertwining of skills and trades typical of the craft workshop with an ancient and deep-rooted organizational practice typical of industrial production.

Another tradition that Italy shares with Germany and, in part, with France also dates back to the low Middle Ages, a tradition that proved strategic precisely in the sector of textiles and apparel: the tradition of period fairs, sites of recurring exchanges of ideas and innovation, essential engines for industries with a seasonal character.

Alfa Romeo Giulia Zagato, 1965

(Farabolafoto)

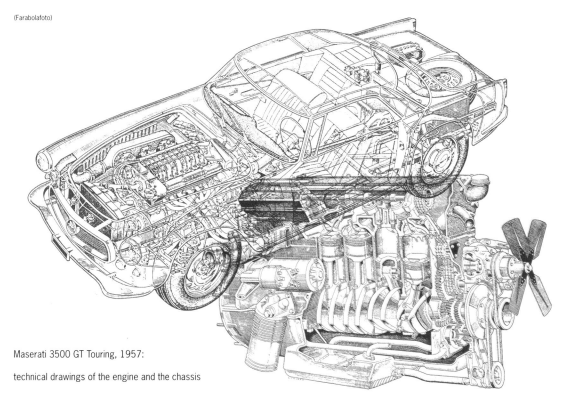

Maserati 3500 GT Touring, 1957:

technical drawings of the engine and the chassis

The Italy that was ahead of its time was succeeded by a long period during which the overall trends were quite the opposite: Italy always seemed to be running behind northwestern Europe. From the seventeenth century until well into the late eighteenth century, Italy seemed to be chained to the past.

This was a weakness that might present some advantages in terms of glamour. Italy in particular was seen as possessing a heritage of ancient and venerable treasures, plundered with the eyes along the ritual tourist routes of the Grand Tour and, later, the Baedeker tours, or literally purloined—at a moderate price—as souvenirs: a country whose finest quality was, perhaps, that it had been left behind, that it had stopped, in a certain sense, in the past. This is the charm of the cities that were great in the fourteenth to sixteenth centuries, and whose development seemed to have ended suddenly at that point: little towns in Umbria or Siena with its giant, unfinished cathedral. And the signs of a country locked in the past, decadent and fascinating because of the decadence, appeared to have a market value throughout the century: from twentieth-century advertisements for Elizabeth Arden that allude to eighteenth-century Venice to modern commercials by Wim Wenders that place the most up-to-date electric appliances in the painterly icons of late mannerism. In the overall image of the country, the modernity ahead of its time still intertwines today with the modernity that failed, and the two do not clash, indeed they feed one upon the other.

A Burning Modernization

In the 1960s and 1970s, a third element was added to the picture, giving a new and different meaning to the other two elements rather than

Soft-Porn all'italiana:
Nino Manfredi and Maria Grazia Buccella
in Vedo Nudo, directed by Dino Risi,
1969

Opposite:
"Autumn: they become women again: major couturiers present their new creations in Rome for the fall/winter 1966 haute couture season," from Epoca, August 1966

suppressing them. This is the modernity of present-day Italy, a modernity unlike any other and yet at the same time apparently exemplary. (In the place of the Italian way to socialism—long theorized by the historic leader of Italian Communism, Palmiro Togliatti—the country has thus discovered what we might well describe as the Italian way to modernity.)

Italy, perhaps of all the Western nations, may be the one that most rapidly and traumatically experienced the leap from a preindustrial and premodern condition to a condition that was fully aligned with—and, indeed, that pioneered—the current characteristics of global production. In order to see the truth of this, a few basic facts should suffice.

In the first postwar census of Italy in 1951 a plurality of the workforce was still involved in farming; thirty years later the statistics on employment broken down by sector were already those of a typical postindustrial economy, with a sharp predominance of the service industry and, especially, of the knowledge-based services. The fully modern phase of the Italian economy, in which industry and factories were not only the most important source of income but also an everyday presence in the lives of most of the population (a phase that in most of the larger western European countries and in the United States lasted at least eighty to a hundred years), went through its entire life cycle in Italy in just thirty years.

Equally rapid, and roughly simultaneous to the process described above, was the secularization of Italy. In the 1950s the majority of Italians were practicing Catholics. That is to say, they did not merely declare their religious faith; they shaped their lives and customs to their religion: from Sunday mass to yearly communion, right down to the bizarre but long-fundamental precept not to eat meat on Fridays (this precept was more widely respected than many other, more important rules, and for decades it dictated the dietary patterns of the nation). Twenty years later, the majority of Italians was still avowedly Catholic, but only

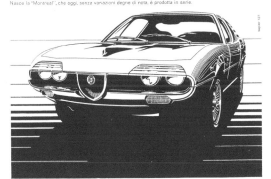

Alfa Romeo Montreal, 1967

Design by Bertone

a minority were practicing Catholics—a sizable minority, but still less than a third of the population; most important, a great many Catholics, whether practicing or not, were no longer willing to obey the church in every matter, even the most ethically charged issues, such as the prohibition of divorce and abortion: the Italians made this abundantly clear in the 1970s in two referendum votes on those matters. Both referendums swept by a secular coalition, beating the church by a thumping majority.

One particularly vivid example of this process of secularization was the massive explosion of pornography—an egotistic form of sexuality, disturbing to many in its brutal vulgarity. Right up to 1968, Italy had a very strict system of censorship, and any publication that showed even a tiny bit of a woman's nipple or any other forbidden anatomical part was subject to immediate confiscation. State television scrupulously avoided not only all nudity in its broadcasts, but even references to adultery and divorce. Over the course of five years, by 1972 or 1973, the situation had changed radically—hard-core pornographic magazines were sold in every newsstand with explicit covers in full public view, and the same is true today.

When the government monopoly on radio and television was shattered in 1975, there were soon shows on the air of an obscenity unrivaled in other countries, beginning with the renowned "striptease of the housewives" broadcast by a private television station in Turin, an unparalleled indicator of the exceedingly rapid slippage of what Italian law calls "the common sense of modesty." Less than twenty years later, many of the Albanians who reached Italy on rafts and freighters during the final spasms of the Communist regime declared that they had been attracted to Italy in part—if not entirely—by the television shows full of naked women. This is not only an image of prosperity but one of total permissiveness, which partly overturns the stereotypes bound up with the country's Catholicism and in part reaffirms the stereotype that has taken root during the twentieth century perhaps more than any other: that of the amoral and pleasantly sensual *dolce vita.*

Perhaps the most significant statistics with regards to Italian modernization are those concerning its demographics. In less than forty years Italy has progressed from being one of the most fertile countries in Europe (roughly even with West Germany) to being the least fertile country in the world: a change that depends upon, and brings with it, a great many other changes, a shift in the attitude toward the future, and a profound transformation of the institution of the family. If the

flight from the countryside and the ensuing rapid conversion to a service economy, the process of secularization, and the exceedingly rapid shift in demographics all serve as a foundation for and at the same time a demonstration of an individualistic Weltanschauung, we can safely say that individualism came about differently in Italy than elsewhere: with the intensity and rapidity of the sloughing of old skin. In the 1950s, it lay in the future, yet to come; in the 1970s it was already ripe.

Icons of Modernization: Cars, Traffic Jams, Appliances in the 1960s

We can see the very instant of this shedding of an old skin, the very brief period in which modernity had its advent in Italy, not so much in the art cinema of Antonioni, Visconti, and others as in the comic movies of the *commedia all'italiana*, and especially in the work of Dino Risi, films that went out of their way to depict the transition, the brief (and tentative) season of modern life in Italy. In *Il Sorpasso* (1962), Vittorio Gassman represents a chameleon shedding its scales while doing everything possible to avoid sensing the trauma, in accordance with the axiom offered in a literary bestseller of those years, *Il Gattopardo* (*The Leopard*) by Tomasi di Lampedusa: "If we want things to stay as they are, things will have to change."

The modernity that lasted a century in the rest of Europe and in the United States had produced, over time, a uniform society (or an apparently uniform society) that consumed mass-market goods, a regimented and clean community, unfailingly presentable—that modernity radically modified the environment without leaving systematic and visible traces of the past, which were gradually removed. In Italy, on the other hand, the aesthetic change in everyday life took place almost entirely in just ten years, from the middle of the 1950s to the middle of the 1960s—there was no time to clear away anything. Nothing is thrown away—huge tenement apartment buildings stand next to the

countryside and sheep pens; thousands and thousands of automobiles go rumbling through millennia-old urban centers; factories are built in the middle of large cities; Lambrettas and Vespas go zipping by, driven by farmers and lawyers. The image of Italy that will be transmitted around the world is that of a place of impossible contrasts, as seen in *Roman Holiday* and *La Dolce Vita*, horrible public housing surrounded by the sheep of Pasolini. What a strange country greets the foreigner's amazed stare, a blessed assembly of beauties and horrors, elegance and filth, that will fill the notebooks of American, British, and German correspondents for decades and decades. In this Italy, the prehistoric grotto dwellings in the rocks of Matera coexist with the elegant architecture of Olivetti, advanced industrial design coexists with premodern nooks and crannies—too many different towns and cities, too many different ages and eras, and an embarrassing lack of community spirit and civic pride, as deplored by Leopardi at least 150 years ago. What kind of modernity is this, where everybody—swollen with pride at their new set of wheels—tries to have a life that is different from that of their neighbors?

The brief modern period in Italy in the 1960s is now a grab bag of images for the world's aesthetic production (consider the Martini advertising campaigns of 1997, or the early Prada collections), a strange case of a revival of the modern. Clearly, it was a mixed modern.

Icons of Afterward: The 1970s

The crucial phase in the Italian passage was the 1970s, not only because many of the transformations we have discussed came to a sort of maturity in the decade, but chiefly because those

Giò Ponti, scale model
for a "finestra ammobiliata," (1954),
Rassegna 58, 1994

"Italia in Lucania," 1981
Photograph by Francesco Radino
Rassegna 58, 1994

transformations became truly and ineluctably visible. The crisis that Italian society was passing through became—perhaps for the first time—the subject of cultural reflection, violently pessimistic and critical in the writings of Pier Paolo Pasolini, or, inversely, drunken on the newness of this unique modernization in the short period of *punk italiano*.

In particular, the 1970s were a time of a mass sociocultural phenomenon: the persistence, for many years, of the youth rebellion that in Italy, as elsewhere in Europe, originated in 1967 and 1968. While it may have achieved little in political terms, the new Italian left of the 1970s was the primordial broth—or laboratory culture—in which a variety of new lifestyles developed, along with a general proliferation of multiple identities, some bound up with ancient traditions (the resurgence of local movements in various parts of the country, at first with a taboo-shattering, vaguely leftist orientation that became, as time went on, increasingly conservative), others avowedly urban and postmodern.

Even compared to other countries, the intelligentsia of the period was ahead of the curve by several years—admittedly with some confusion—in terms of its perception of the crisis of the world of mass production and the assembly line, the growth of mass intellectualism, and the abolition of the rigorous separation between work time and leisure time. While the world seemed to have become a living inferno in the chief Italian cities (these were the so-called years of lead, a time of terrorism, when the cover of *Der Spiegel* depicted Italy with a photograph of a pistol lying on a plate of spaghetti), in the northern provinces—in the industrial districts that economists and sociologists were just beginning to recognize as such—completely innovative models of production, flexible and individual, were being tested. While the magazines in Germany were mainly concerned that terrorism might ruin their Italian holidays,

Assembly of washing machines at the

Candy factory, Brugherio, Milan, 1965

(Publifoto Olympia)

Opposite:

The low point in the media image of Italy:

cover of the German newsweekly Der Spiegel,

25 July, 1977

(Courtesy Der Spiegel)

Giorgio Armani on the cover of Time, representing

the definitive success of Italian fashion on the world

scene and marking a relaunching of the

"Italian national system," 1982

(Courtesy Giorgio Armani Spa)

American magazines dedicated attention to fashion; in 1982 Giorgio Armani appeared on the cover of *Time*. And, in fact, it was during the 1970s that—on the interior of a manufacturing sector with ancient roots, the sector of textiles and apparel—there began to spring up new styles and new figures, the very styles and figures that still distinguish Italian style. The links between the larger transformations of the period and the new developments of fashion are not difficult to identify. Italy's strange modernization proved to be strategic (though in an entirely unplanned manner) to the image of the country, especially in terms of fashion: the setting of a short circuit between past and future, singularly self-aware, and at the same time fissured by dark, vague lines of desperation, a model of modernization that is at once quite special and yet intuitively easy to grasp.

It is a non-linear, hybrid model, where nothing is discarded. If in the past few years the rejection of modernity has been shaking up the most advanced European nations, and even the United States, with waves of revisionism and painful confessions, if the cost of modern cleanliness is proving painful for many, the reader may perhaps understand from this analysis the way in which Italy's lack of harmony, its closed synchronicity have proven—to the surprise of one and all, and entirely by chance—a strangely efficacious way of surviving in contingent time.

Milano ● 02138

Richard Martin

In the fall of 1989, the zip code of men's tailoring became 02138, that of Harvard Square in Cambridge, Massachusetts. Following a series of tentative appreciations of the Ivy League sack suit, its long, droopy look prevailed and was announced by Alexander Lobrano in a front-page article in *DNR* (January 17, 1989): "The revival of the Ivy League Sack Suit began in Florence among young men's Pitti exhibitors and has been gradually accepted by such large manufacturers as Reporter over the course of the last few seasons." In fashion's propensity to evolve—as opposed to the specious common wisdom that fashion only hurls forward with innovation—the shaped, two-button suit was overwhelmed by the rally of interest in the flaccid, three-button model, largely unfamiliar in advanced fashion since 1960 and often the scapegoat of preppy nonchalance and conservatism.

In the United States, the liberal-conservative dialectic was especially vivid: the conservative presidential candidate of 1960, Richard M. Nixon, who, never debonair, wore three-button suits at the time, lost the election to the two-button, shaped suit that styled the liberal, social, and sartorial charisma of John F. Kennedy. For the fall of 1989, the new tailored look from Giorgio Armani was proclaimed throughout the market as the sack suit. Its name was resonant with American campuses and might have seemed at first to represent an authority and sartorial guide displaced to the United States. The full chest, narrow lapels, widely spaced stripes, and boxy silhouette of the Armani suit for fall 1989, as photographed for *DNR*, comprise the epitome of the Ivy League favorite with one notable exception. The full trousers betray the Ivy League of the 1950s and reach back farther into

Moschino Jeans
advertising campaign,
fall/winter 1990-91
Photograph by Stefano Pandini
(Courtesy Moschino Spa)

Opposite:
Giorgio Armani advertising campaign,
fall/winter 1998-99
Photograph by Aldo Fallai
(Courtesy Giorgio Armani Spa)

sartorial history to the Oxford bags, popular not only at Oxford but also favored as leisure trousers on American campuses of the 1920s. But does the look of fall 1989 rest on the American icon, or simply pause at the usurpation, in part by coincidence and in part by cognizance? Does the look evolve rapidly and dynamically into something else, an Italian icon of the men's suit that replaces the power suit of the 1980s, itself an Italian icon of global domination?

It is, of course, clear that men's tailoring takes its address for the fall semester of 1989 as 02138, the American campus; but forward fashion immediately takes its forwarding address as Italy, all but annihilating those first campus looks. This transfiguration in Italian fashion is, of course, very different from the stable veneration of Ivy League style in Japan, where the sack suit and other elements of Ivy style endure unchanged. For Italy, longer, leaner lines replaced the sack as early as spring-summer 1990. Even such menswear designers as Romeo Gigli, who had been making boxy jackets for several years, lengthened the jacket and keep the pants tight. By spring 1990, three-button suits or jackets were prevalent, but those designers employing them, such as Franco Moschino, were shaping and cropping the jackets unlike any Ivy League style. For spring 1990, only Giorgio Armani was showing a classic three-button sack with broad natural shoulders, wide sleeves, and capacious pants. But, as always, Armani showed so many looks, from chalk-striped business suits to double-

breasted suits, and was offering so many messages on the runway that the solo figure in the sack suit might be lost in the mix. If there was one discernible Harvard man on the runway, he was simply caught up in the spectacle of menswear that was offered in the late 1980s after black Monday and in the waning of the power suit. By fall 1990, elements of Ivy were as much at home on the Italian runways as in the red leather lounge chairs of the Yale Club. But Italian menswear was shrewdly separating and dispersing the component parts—three-button jacket, boxy natural-shouldered jacket, and

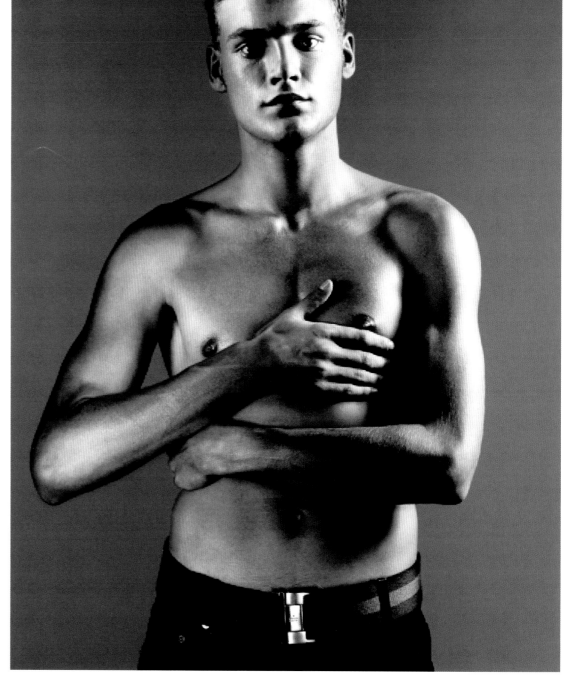

Gucci advertising campaign,
fall/winter 1998-99
Photograph by Steven Klein
(Courtesy Gucci spa)

Opposite:
"Sandro," Alessandro Raho, 1997,
oil on canvas, 259 x 183 cm.
(Courtesy Maureen Paley Interim Art, London)

untapered trousers—and using all three independently. For Dolce & Gabbana, for example, leisure pants re-created the example of Oxford bags and even exaggerated the effect with paper-bag waists cinched with leather belts. Three-button suits by Dolce & Gabbana still had some shaping and lapels much wider than those of an archetypal Ivy League look. A comprehensive process of assimilation was underway: Dolce & Gabbana for fall 1990 looked not Ivy League but wholly distinctive, having absorbed the American style by components, even those components that were slightly mixed and anachronistic in fall 1989. A year later, these are elements of style, Italian style.

In fact, what happens to the Ivy style in the 1990s might be thought, in a literal sense, to be an indignity to Harvard Yard, J. Press, and Brooks Brothers, as the style is continuously adapted and reinvented to become Italian style. The sack suit—with variations in the 1920s and 1950s—is to be preserved forever by some as an inflexible and unchanging standard in dress and in values. One need only visit one of the American university clubs to recognize that the sack suit, along with the rep tie and the Oxford button-down-collar shirt have not changed for at least forty years. This American icon will never change, even when managing to defy its parody and permutations in class and quality offered by Ralph Lauren in the 1970s and 1980s. This American icon will never change, even as an acute analysis of its parts fostered the new look in Italian menswear in the 1990s.

(Let's not awaken the sleeping alumni in their leather armchairs; they would rather not know, and they will never buy Gucci.) The fate of sack-suit elements or gestures, more taken individually than as a whole, has been prodigious in Italian menswear of the 1980s. The natural-shouldered jacket of longer length has been taken to every possible variation, including compromises with outerwear coats, extreme appearances of length in skinny four- and five-button single-breasted silhouettes, the longer torso line of double-breasted silhouettes buttoning on two, and jackets—including a revival of the Nehru jacket—with fly-front closures that obviate the counting of buttons. Inevitably, the sack suit's proportions encourage narrow lapels of the kind Italy has unrelentingly explored in the 1990s, after a decade of substantive lapels. The full trousers that appeared as an anomalous part of the Ivy League ensemble in 1989 have become recurrent in Italian tailored menswear through the early 1990s and in sportswear continuously, allowing for a variety of materials in the bold swagger of what had begun as the slightly ludicrous Oxford bags, but which Italian fashion tends to discipline into handsome trousers with pleated waists.

In a simple comparison, consider the differences between the editorial content of the July-August 1988 *L'Uomo Vogue* and the same magazine for July-August 1998. Like any review in a menswear magazine, a remarkable amount remains the same or similar. The salient differences reside in proportions. In 1988, most jackets button directly about the waist, allowing for great expanses of shirts, ties, layered sweaters, waist-coats or vests, turtlenecks, or scarves, as pursued with abandon by the stylists. Some trousers are baggy, but for the most part they are tapered. To our eyes today, many of the jackets appear short, though a long jacket and a long wool coat by Corneliani are featured in an article on dandies.

Ten years later, in 1998, the effect of the Ivy transfiguration is obvious. Suits are three-button, have a fly front, and close very high, allowing for a very high gorge and minimal exposure of shirt and tie. Shirts and ties are prone, as we know, to dark complementary colors that all but disappear into the jacket. On the editorial pages, trousers are not baggy, but neither are they conspicuously tapered; a number of short coats double as jackets. In fact, the dozen plus men in black on the cover all wear white shirts with collars under dark suits, virtually every one of high gorge closing at the sternum or above, showing three or more buttons buttoned or the ambiguity of a fly front, and trousers that are of a true 1950s tightness. Dour, indeed, in photography, but these clean-cut men, largely with classic American looks and conservative haircuts, could have been plucked from Harvard Square in 1955. It is no longer Rembrandt's image of burghers, nor is it Harvard's pride. It is now—rightly—an Italian icon.

Of course, this story of 1990s menswear only recapitulates the oft-told tale of Italian postwar women's clothing having seized American sportswear, just as Seventh Avenue lost faith in its native design talent and skulked back to the thralldom of Paris under Dior and Balenciaga in the 1950s and 1960s. Italy produced luxury sportswear—answering to contemporary ways of life but using the finest materials—of the kind that America invented in the 1940s and 1950s, but faltered in producing when Americans chose to be subservient to Paris again in the 1950s and 1960s. The American origins quickly became obscure in the short memory of fashion, and Italy made high-quality sportswear a distinctively Italian icon of the 1970s and 1980s. That well-known paradigm was repeated in the 1990s, when what began as campus style in America and was even acknowledged as such at its emergence in 1989 became, in fashion's ability to alter and create, the great Italian icon of menswear in the 1990s.

Opposite:

Gianfranco Ferrè advertising campaign,

spring/summer 1999

Photograph by Don Cunningham

(Courtesy Gianfranco Ferrè Spa)

The Italian·Mile

Manhattan

Soho

5th Avenue

Madison Avenue

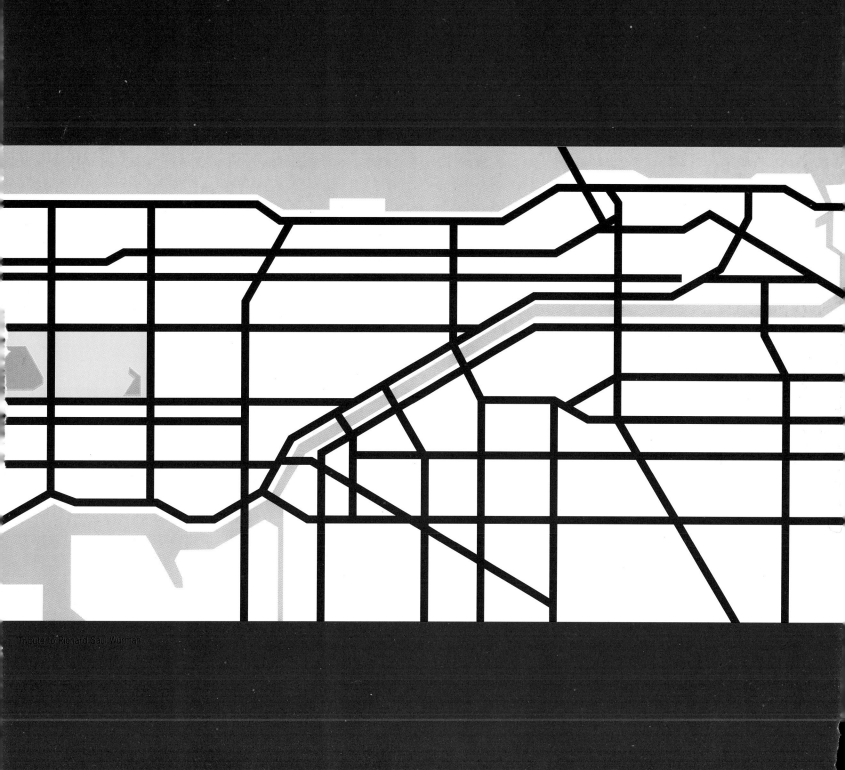

Tribute to Richard Saul Wurman

Giannino Malossi
Photo Leslie Fratkin

In the stretch of Manhattan between Fiftieth Street and Seventieth Street, along Fifth Avenue and Madison Avenue, in the heart of the city of New York, Italian identity finds a formidable source of expression, determined by the specific density of shops selling the creations of Italian fashion designers. Downtown, between Houston Street and West Broadway, the same scene is repeated. Thus, the visibility of Italian fashion has made it possible for New York City to attain a long-cherished ambition—to become a world fashion capital. In return, the presence of Italian fashion in New York projects the icon of Italy into a light of high prestige around the world, legitimizing its importance as a vehicle for the expression of global culture.

The Italian Look

Valerie Steele

Except for "pasta and opera, the Italians can't be credited with anything," insisted Pierre Bergé, the business partner of French designer Yves Saint Laurent. A journalist from *Time* magazine had asked him about Italian fashion and, in particular, about Giorgio Armani. Apparently this struck a nerve. "Give me one piece of clothing, one fashion statement that Armani has made that has truly influenced the world," demanded Bergé. It was a rash challenge to make to an American journalist (who had probably chosen to interview Bergé in the hope that he would criticize Armani), and in his article Jay Cocks impudently replied, "Alors, Pierre. The unstructured jacket. An easeful elegance... Tailoring of a kind thought possible only when done by hand... A new sort of freedom in clothes."

This story reveals a great deal about American attitudes toward French versus Italian fashion. Americans have long felt deeply ambivalent about French fashion: are Parisian couturiers artistic geniuses or pretentious dictators? American perceptions of Italian fashion, however, are almost uniformly positive. Indeed, American coverage of Italian fashion has focused on the way it combines the casual ease of American sportswear with European luxury and status. As *Esquire* once put it, Italian designers provide a "rich, relaxed style." In fact, many fashion-conscious Americans have found an idealized self-image in the Italian look.

The Italian look needs to be distinguished from Italian fashion per se. Italian-made clothes have never comprised more than a small percentage of the clothes sold on the American market. Beyond percentages and sales figures, however, lie the high prestige and widespread influence of the Italian

Opposite:

Gianni Versace advertising campaign,

spring/summer 1994

Photograph by Richard Avedon

(Courtesy Gianni Versace Spa)

Opposite:

Dolce & Gabbana advertising campaign,

spring/summer 1988

Photograph by Ferdinando Scianna

(Courtesy Dolce & Gabbana Spa)

look—which has increasingly displaced the Anglophile Brooks Brothers style from its formerly preeminent position. As Chiara Giannelli Buss argues, "The concept of 'Made in Italy,' hitherto the guarantee of fine materials, excellent workmanship and good taste [was replaced] with that of the 'Italian look,' the status symbol of a new economic power, conscious of the social implications of fashion and with a decidedly international character."

Italy's international image was partly a reflection of the Italian films of the 1950s, which frequently showcased Italian fashion. Italian style was also perceived through the lens of international high society. Recognized for the quality of its materials and workmanship, Italian clothes were sought after by fastidious clients, such as the Duke of Windsor. By 1960, there was also a significant Italian influence on London's young, mod styles. As David Bowie recalled: "I liked Italian stuff . . . the box jackets and the mohair." Other Italian products, such as the Vespa motor scooter, also functioned as classic icons of modern design.

Important as these developments were, however, they remained largely in the realm of material objects "Made in Italy." The Italian look, as such, did not truly emerge until the 1970s, concurrent with the rise of the Italian ready-to-wear industry based in Milan. By the end of the decade the Italian uprising seriously threatened French fashion hegemony. "Weary of French fantasy clothes and rude treatment on Parisian showroom floors, buyers were happy to take their order books next

door," reported *Newsweek*. The clothes coming out of Milan were, admittedly, not couture, but they were extremely stylish. "They were classically cut but not stodgy: innovative but never theatrical," declared *Newsweek*. "They were for real people—albeit rich people—to wear to real places."

Milan offered a genuine alternative to Paris. American fashion journalists proclaimed the good news that Milan produced "casual, relaxed clothes," which seemed to be "shaping up as a variant on the American sportswear look." The United States has its own sportswear industry, of course. But because American clothes are produced for a mass market, they tend to lack the style and production quality of Italian clothes. "The Italians were the first to make refined sportswear," recalled John Fairchild, the publisher of *Women's Wear Daily*. "Americans don't mind spending, if the sweater is by Krizia or Missoni." Moreover, he added, "The best fabrics in the world are Italian, [so] Italy starts off at an advantage."

The Italian look also "came to bridge the gap between the anti-Establishment 1960's and the money-gathering 1980's," as fashion writer Woody Hochswender astutely observed. Much of the initial popularity of the Armani suit, for example, derived from its image as the suit that was not really a suit, or rather that carried the power and prestige of a suit without being stiff or square. In place of rigidly tailored business suits, symbolizing rectitude and bourgeois masculinity, Italian designers such as Armani gradually introduced softer jackets without padding and stiff interlinings. The shoulders dropped and broadened, the lapels and buttons crept downward. Colors became more subtle and

Opposite:

Giorgio Armani advertising campaign, fall/winter 1998-99

Photograph by Paolo Roversi

(Courtesy Giorgio Armani Spa)

androgynous, fabrics softer and more luxurious. "Armani disarmed men and their clothes erotically without unmanning them," wrote American journalist Judith Thurman. "He freed them to be looked at and desired by women (and other men)." The protagonist in *American Gigolo* dressed exclusively in Armani, and, according to Thurman, "His shopping trips provided the film's true sexual excitement." No sooner had Armani feminized and eroticized menswear than he interpreted his menswear look for the modern businesswoman, emphasizing the power of androgyny. By skillfully exploiting the use of soft, easily draped luxury fabrics for their tactile appeal, Armani created clothes that eschewed phallic hardness in favor of satisfying what Freud called "the libido for touching."

Gianni Versace, of course, became the most famous exponent of sexually expressive clothing for both men and women. Especially influential was his use of leather, a material that carries connotations of radical sexuality. Versace's brilliantly colored silk shirts featuring a baroque exuberance of design also openly positioned men as sex objects and reinforced the Anglo-Saxon stereotype of the Latin lover. His women's clothes were even more seductive. As Richard Martin observes, "Versace chose as his heroic female model the prostitute or streetwalker" transfigured into media star.

The contrasting paradigms of Armani and Versace are reinscribed on the next generation of Italian designers. "Cool Rises to Intimidating Heights," announced the *New York Times* in an article on Miuccia Prada. Famous for the refined opulence of her creations, Prada epitomizes the modern deluxe style associated with Milan. Her austere

artistry has become the focus of a veritable cult of fashionistas, whose designs draw on the northern Italian tradition of having discreetly elegant clothes beautifully made by local tailors and dressmakers. Prada herself has emphasized the importance of fabric, and of creating clothing that takes full advantage of Italy's artisan tradition.

Very different is the warm, voluptuous femininity espoused by the design team of Domenico Dolce and Stefano Gabbana. "This partnership revives the Southern Italian sex bomb look, inspired by the ... fiery beauty of stars like Sophia Loren and Gina Lollobrigida." Their menswear also draws on imagery made famous in the films of Roberto Rossellini, Luchino Visconti, and Federico Fellini. Equally important is the clothing's tactile appeal, which implicitly identifies the wearer as sensitive and vulnerable, as well as masculine and powerful.

Thus, Italian style has come to be "perceived as being in the realm of values." Not only are there fine quality clothes "Made in Italy," there also exists a conceptual category known as the "Italian look," which is internationally recognized as a signifier of refined opulence and deluxe modernity, of casual, expensive, sexy elegance. Yet within this general category, there is room for a variety of individual styles, each of which apparently expresses some aspect of what foreigners perceive as *la dolce vita*.

Opposite:

Prada advertising campaign, fall/winter 1998

Photograph by Norbert Schoerner

(Courtesy Prada Spa)

Italian Fashion and the Air-Conditioned Nightmare

Franco La Cecla

To the women of Canton or Beijing, who can finally come and shop in Hong Kong, it must seem like a dream come true to be able to emulate their compatriots, residents of the former British colony. Clustering along the enormous glass-lined corridors of the multistory shopping malls in the quarters of central Hong Kong or Wan Chai, they move from one display window to the next, looking at the leading labels of Europe and America and buying in half an hour what most affluent Hong Kong women couldn't afford in a month. Dozens of outfits by Versace, Ferrè, Prada, and Valentino are offered to the sophisticated women of Hong Kong, who instead have set off in pursuit of more refined, elite-oriented consumption, preferring to shop in stores that sell a few, select, exceedingly expensive products with famous labels that are not too widely seen.

In the period following the handover of Hong Kong—which went from British protectorate to autonomous territory of the People's Republic of China—the fashion that is sold here changed its end consumers, but it remained one of the most powerful images of true wealth. The new China (still flourishing economically despite the Asian crisis) sees Hong Kong not only as a goose that lays golden eggs, and therefore absolutely sacrosanct as a fundamental financial resource, but also as a place that symbolizes a certain type of consumption, which the nouveaux riches of the Chinese mainland are beginning to demand as a status symbol. European fashion, and especially Italian fashion, are a fundamental component of the new face of wealth. The emperor seems to be badly in need of new clothes and, totally uninterested in the moral of the fable by Hans Christian Andersen, he goes in search of clothing made as far as possible from the imperial palace—he goes to Italy.

Italian fashion is so prestigious in Hong Kong that there are many local clothing manufacturers that prefer to appear with Italian name, label, and advertising campaign. Thus, there is a Satchi Italy—which has nothing Italian about it—as well as Giordano, Bossini, Nora Donna, and many other

Opposite:

Hong Kong

Photograph by Michel Setboun

(Grazia Neri)

Hong Kong labels with fake Italian names. Some of these—like Bossini—imitate an Italian logo (the old Benetton logo) and target successfully (at times more successfully than the actual Italian label they are imitating) the same market share.

Fashion in Hong Kong constitutes a separate city, with its own system of shopping malls—marble fixtures, escalators, glass-enclosed elevators, and fountains (but not a place to sit down anywhere!)—polished to a fine glow and spotlessly clean. These are veritable air-conditioned temples filling four or five stories of the skyscrapers belonging to Chinese multinational corporations or banks or to the richest men on earth. These are symbols of the new, unbridled, "cool" Asian capitalism. You can spend a whole day walking from one mall to another along the enormous hanging corridors that link them. The unimaginably wealthy women of Hong Kong never touch the ground; they travel from their air-conditioned homes to their cars with tinted windows to the escalators of the huge shopping centers. They know perfectly well

that there is nothing that expresses their condition of untouchable privilege like Italian and European style. The forty-year-old women of Hong Kong, immobile like porcelain figurines, resembling their country cousins from Beijing only in physical appearance, buy a new Ferrè every week and discard two Prada outfits a month. They preside over glittering "Italian-style" $90,000-a-seat benefit tea parties and ceremonial dinners.

Here fashion is the anti-city, a place where the people with money purchase the right not to have the city made up of streets, sidewalks, traffic, and sweltering heat. The entire city suffers from conditionosis; it is an air-conditioned nightmare whereby the outdoors is unbelievably hot (in a city on the sea, with high mountains behind it, and therefore a potential earthly paradise), and indoors, in the malls, it is ice cold. Fashion is the display window of these interiors, and it is truly the dernier cri of the big money that rules here. This unbridled capital needs—now like never before, and here more

than anywhere else—image and facade and clothing and labels and cool glamour.

Fashion, sealed up in the sterile atmosphere of Hong Kong skyscrapers, has once again become a phantasmagoria of merchandise, as it was in the arcades of Paris described by Walter Benjamin, with the added consideration that even the poor are allowed to stroll through these chilly boulevards of marble and glass, designed by architects such as Foster and Pei.

The most disturbing image is that of the Filipino housekeepers who stroll, by the tens of thousands, through the corridors linking one mall to another, mythologizing their passage in front of certain display windows, thrilling to the spectacle of immense wealth and designer clothing. The poor stroll and strut before this glittering show, confirming its glamour, just like the faceless audience of a television star's show.

Certainly none of this is news; the fact remains, however, that in Hong Kong there is nothing but display window after display window, or else a city that is hot, unbearably hot and filthy. It is as if this were the new face of the planet. Fashion seems to be the only alternative to the earth's devastation, in the sense that fashion exists to tell people that beauty is no longer to be found in nature and in the city but only in the entirely artificial world of consumer goods. The impression is that the success of Italian style is actually not a deeply rooted, long-standing phenomenon, but, rather, what was required for a form of capitalism that has borrowed its aesthetic ideal in order to obliterate the world outside. In this sense, Italy here is an abstract form of exoticism, but it is also the epitome of superiority.

What does fashion really represent today? And what does Italian fashion represent, in particular? Certainly it represents the highest reaches of wealth; it is the status symbol of the achievement of separateness because it is based on distance. Here in Asia, Italy is distant, a country that is as occidental as any other. But what about elsewhere?

If wealth is a facade condition (as well as a condition of actual substance), proper maintenance of the facade means showing the surface, the outfit, in the most glittering manner possible. Fashion is the end of understatement, the end of wealth that prefers not to be seen. That is why fashion is so astonishingly postmodern; the newly wealthy prefer not to keep all that glitters to themselves. They desire an audience to watch them, giving the impression that in some way they assent to their splendor.

It is probable that in this phase of world capitalism, the old Anglo-Saxon models of clothing or the traditional models of samurai managers or mandarin executives no longer work. There is a void in the transition from a colonial world to a postcolonial world. The new wealth—which springs from places that were traditionally closed to outside influences, and that had developed their own codes and customs, without the slightest pretense of universality—is no longer able to identify with the image of the rich person from the 1920s and 1930s. Even if those

Hong Kong

Photograph by Simon Fraser

Science Photo Library, London

(Grazia Neri)

who work in the stock market in Hong Kong and do not sleep at night in order to get the latest figures from the New York Stock Exchange are forced to wear Church shoes and white shirts with a regimental tie, this image no longer holds up once they leave the Hong Kong Stock Exchange.

There is a need for a new international language, and it is available only in the world of fashion. Versace, Armani, Valentino, and Prada all offer—along with the leading labels from France and America—a way of filling this void. They are the international language, the globalizing face of a new wealth that has not yet established its own customs and lifestyles (and that quite often is supertraditional and fundamentalist and conservative—the women of Hong Kong are not much luckier than their cousins from Beijing, who have to put up with concubines and the nearly total lack of rights for women) but at least needs a way of displaying itself. We do not know that this will last. What is certain is that the more unsure of itself the new wealth may be—like the new Chinese wealth, which is just beginning to deal with the problem of how to dress in public—the more it will feel the need to adopt fashion as a style.

We should open a brief parenthesis here concerning the fact that the way that fashion is used in the settings of new wealth is not the same way that this same fashion is used in the places where it is created. While the style of the wealthy in Asia is becoming a vital matter for the holders of capital—who feel a need to justify their existence with a curtain of guaranteed designer elegance—in America and Europe there is a veil of irony (perhaps a false patina, and perhaps a residual trace of Renaissance humanism) whereby fashion is not directly linked to a status symbol, and in some sense a fashion is already a reference to fashion. You can prove that

you are rich by purchasing Italian fashion, but it is not the suit itself that describes your wealth and specifies your social standing (even if it is true that Italian fashion is rather moderate and understated, free of frenzy, and therefore acceptable to the nouveaux riches in search of a dignified image, whether they come from Nigeria or Beijing).

There is, in short, a kind of coolness to Italian fashion, and to fashion in general. In Italy's lines of clothing, there is more than just a consecration of the classical; there is also a subtle irony concerning the fact that an outfit could be so important. Fashion, in this sense, is generally blasé, and it plays with the double face of being apparently meaningless, even though it alludes to enormous privileges. This apparent ironic and democratic openness of fashion constitutes the foundation of its accessibility as a language to many levels of society. It may well connote a rich woman from Hong Kong, but it remains appetizing to a poor Filipino housekeeper. These are no longer the outfits that princes, kings, and queens might wear; they are outfits that fully announce their fugacity and futility, their evanescence and uselessness. In this sense they fit perfectly with a disposable idea of fashion, in which an outfit is just a glittering disguise, a perfect counterpoint to the marble fittings of a multinational office building.

This is true in Hong Kong, just as it is true in New York, Miami, Paris, or Sydney. Italian style, in any case, lies in this new face of wealth, which needs to declare to the world that there is a form of beauty that can be purchased, but only at a very high price—and that this form of beauty consists, precisely, in a question of style. Italian style, nowadays, is something so automatic in the minds of millions of consumers around the world that it is difficult to give anything but an intuitive description of it. There is

a certain way of life that is hinted at by certain outfits and to an even greater degree, by certain atmospheres bound up with advertising campaigns, labels, and evocative names. Italy is—increasingly—fashion, but especially something that should be immediately understood by anyone who truly comprehends the *bella vita*, or fine life.

It is strange that an idea developed at the end of the 1960s, around a world that has since vanished completely—the idea of the Italian *dolce vita*—should have survived and traveled the world as it has done, right up to the present day. If the film *Roman Holiday*, with Gregory Peck and Audrey Hepburn, still constitutes for the Japanese the first image that they associate with Italy, and if the *arte di vivere* continues to be the prime stereotype for non-Italians of everyday life in Italy, this means that the Italian dream has taken root outside of Italy with astonishing vigor. It is a dream that has transcended itself, becoming a long-term stereotype. The most refined rich people may grow weary of it, of course, because it is now anything but a progressive dream; it is a form of nostalgia (perhaps a yearning for a Piazza Navona style that never existed).

Even for Italians the dream seems a bit outdated. Would we still recognize ourselves in the stereotypes of Italy as the land of *la dolce vita* and *il dolce far niente*? Of course not—the country in which we live is light years away from that old dream. What is happening is that the dream is whipping back at us like a boomerang, in the sense that the Italian style that is successful outside of Italy is beginning to establish itself as a stereotype among the Italians themselves. For the first time, the Italians are beginning to realize that there is an identity, a specific Italian icon, whose outlines and features are more familiar to non-Italians than to the

Italians themselves. But if the Italians of the 1960s and 1970s could laugh, or at least smile, at themselves with Vittorio De Sica, Alberto Sordi, and Ugo Tognazzi, the attitude is not the same today.

Do the Italians really know what they look like? And if so, does this identity have anything to do with the ability to produce facades and status symbols for the wealthy of the world? There are no clear answers to these questions, but it is interesting that they should arise at a moment of transition in Italian history, when there is a perception of certain stereotypes of the national identity, but no genuine nostalgia.

Someone should examine the question of why the Italians are given so little to nostalgia about their own "the way we were." It may be that it is a nation that is still too young to look back in longing. Nostalgia for the way the Italians once were, if anything, comes to us from outside of Italy. And it is funny to think that—because of a trick apparently accomplished with mirrors—the Italians buy suits that have a nostalgic look, produced in Germany or Asia, concerning a past that they don't miss in the slightest.

If the success of the image of Italy outside of Italy is entirely a result of the aura that fashion has managed to create around itself, then we should say that the Italians have no choice but to keep quiet and enjoy the results. To reveal that the real situation does not correspond to the dream would not be hygienic. But what does this dream actually consist of, and how will it affect the Italians of the present day (and is it already beginning to boomerang)?

The dream imagines a country where style is an elevated conception of how one presents oneself as well as a way of being, in the sense that outside of Italy the Italians are thought of as the people with the greatest control over the relationship between clothing and behavior—a certain undefinable way of being and appearing that fascinates the nouveaux riches and the nouveaux très riches of the world. And it also fascinates the poor, given that

the society of the spectacle could not exist without an audience and that consumerism is nothing more than a need for an audience for the big money. How much of this whole issue of fashion is having repercussions—and will continue to have repercussions—in Italy? A great deal, because fashion is truly becoming the only unifying image for a country such as Italy that is still struggling to find a coherent way of depicting itself. Pasta, pizza, Venice, Rome, Milan, but especially fashion.

Italy after Shenzhen is an Italy that knows only what it is not. It is not America, because the American way of life is exotic to an Italian; nor is it part of the managerial and industrial image of Europe. Italy, then, is a country that looks upon style as a resource, but it is not clear where that style is now. Because the landscape has been largely destroyed, the *dolce vita* has gone away, and if fragments of good living (*bel vivere*) survive, they are sorely tried by an overall situation of deterioration and pollution. Italian cities are no less intolerable than other large, polluted, and traffic-choked cities around the world, and everyday life can no longer avail itself of the street and other public places as theaters in which to display oneself.

Fashion, perhaps, provides an opportunity to stop for a moment and think about the origins of Italian style. And what if we discover that the origin lies precisely in that culture, that system of values and motivations with which a society makes sense of its everyday existence, that culture that has expressed itself in art, food, landscape, and ways of interacting? Then Italy might awaken from its long sleep and realize that the source of so much great wealth, which comes to us from around the world, is a fragile structure, subject to decay, but still possible to save.

The Wooing of Italy

Antony Shugaar

Christopher Columbus started it all, by sensing that America existed. Nothing could be more romantic than that stirring of the soul, that indefinable westward yearning that led Columbus to America. It is the stuff of puppy love—twin souls, fated to meet. This special elective affinity has bound Italy and America ever since. Of course, this indefinable bond linking them—which we shall attempt to define here—is only one factor in the overall relationship.

There are any number of other, real factors: a certain Italian tradition of industrial craftsmanship, Italy's expertise in managing style as a standardized product, an enormous national artistic heritage, a vast flow of high-end tourism, culinary excellence that is universally regarded. Despite all that, there is an unmistakably romantic aspect to the intercultural wooing and reciprocal yearning that goes on between the two nations.

We might ask—quoting an old song—how long has this been going on? In fact, the terms of this affair have remained pretty much constant over the centuries: Italy plays the ever ardent suitor; America is the blushing, flattered, buxom country wench (proudly bearing the name of an Italian map maker, a map maker she'll never forget).

And the yearning that stirred Columbus's heart? That was actually an old line, borrowed from an even greater Italian than Columbus: Dante Alighieri, fully seven hundred years ago, imagined a little chat with the eternally damned soul of Ulysses, who told of sailing west beyond the Pillars of Hercules, out onto the broad Atlantic. Ulysses, in *terza rima*: "'O brothers,' I said, 'who through a hundred thousand perils have reached the

west . . . do not deny the experience, following the sun, of the world without people . . . You were not made to live like brutes, but to follow virtue and knowledge.'"

Perhaps only an irrepressible optimist could equate America with "virtue and knowledge," but even in *The Divine Comedy*, the founding work of Italian culture, there is an almost atavistic yen for the New World to the west.

Stereotypes have been much maligned in recent years. This is understandable; they are baseless unless taken for what they are: tropes, or habits, of cultural dynamics. The idea of Italian passion and fervent courtship, for instance, is foolish if seen as an inborn, genetically transmitted trait; less foolish if seen as a cultural and economic tactic, persistent over time. Thus, to quote Gina Lollobrigida's memorable distinction: "In Hollywood, they bring you ice-cold Coke to show you're a regular guy . . . But in Italy they bring you nothing—they are too busy kissing your arms." And the New World, flattered and blushing, never fails to respond. The matter of continuity in cultural patterns bears some exploration.

The late Lynn T. White Jr. wrote—in a 1965 essay entitled "The Legacy of the Middle Ages in the American Wild West"— "A blind spot in the study of the history of the United States is the failure to recognize our detailed and massive continuity with the European Middle Ages . . . Indeed, a good case could be made for the thesis that today the United States is closer to the Middle Ages than is Europe."

White—a noted scholar of medieval technology and society—cites the log cabin (a typical medieval building technique in Scandinavia), the stockade fort (a wooden mimesis of the medieval walled town), the covered wagon (a direct descendant of the twelfth-century *caretta longa*), the stagecoach, barbed wire, the horizontal-axle windmill, whiskey, playing cards (the ancient Romans used dice, not cards), and even hanging (it was a medieval innovation to execute by hanging; in ancient times it was a method of suicide, used notably by Judas Iscariot). Once something gets started in a culture, White is saying, it tends to continue—until displaced by something more deeply rooted. The point is how deeply rooted—and unreasoning—our basic fondness for things Italian may be.

An even more instructive indicator of cultural and technological continuity can be found in the U.S. standard railroad gauge, or space between track rails: 4 feet 8½ inches, decidedly an odd number. The American gauge derives from the English gauge; the English one from the gauge of pre-steam tramways; those in turn copied the spacing of wooden wagon wheels. It's like the old song about the bones: those wooden wagon wheels were made to fit the ruts on old Roman roads; to do otherwise would have risked damage on the stone roads. Those ruts were made by Roman war chariots, which were built to standard military specifications, with a gauge of 4 feet 8½ inches. That gauge? It derived from the width of a pair—or span—of horses. Thus, the track gauge of the newest American bullet train was originally determined by the physical size of ancient beasts of burden. Once a pattern is set, it is hard to shake it. And the commonly held American opinion— and admiration—of Italy is as ancient, and as self-perpetuating, as the rut in a Roman road. It has persisted, renewing itself with each generation, for much of this millennium.

"Travel is the ruin of all happiness! There's no looking at a building here after seeing Italy," wrote the English novelist and diarist Fanny Burney in 1782. Around the same time, Samuel Johnson said: "A man who has not been in Italy, is always conscious of an inferiority, from his not having seen what it is expected a man should see." Charles V— who, after all, owned much of Italy and a good portion of Europe—understood a fundamental and age-old portion of Italy's appeal: the sexiness of its language and style. "To God I speak Spanish, to women Italian, to men French, and to my horse—German." Mark Twain, who sensed a sacred cow when he saw one, burst out impatiently in 1869: "Lump the whole thing! say that the Creator made Italy from designs by Michael Angelo!" And Truman Capote might have been speaking about Italy as a whole when he said: "Venice is like eating an entire box of chocolate liqueurs in one go." Italy, like anything fashionable, has gone out of fashion now and again in America. There was a time—from the turn of the century until the end of World War II—when Italy was looked upon with suspicion and fear. It was a time of Italian truculence and American insularity. Those Italians who were not busy being truculent in Italy migrated in vast numbers to America from 1880 to 1930, both triggering and ultimately breaking down the vast American insularity of 1910 to 1930.

Familiarity, they say, breeds contempt, and by the time Sinclair Lewis lampooned American xenophobia in *Babbitt*, Italians had become quite familiar and were held in some

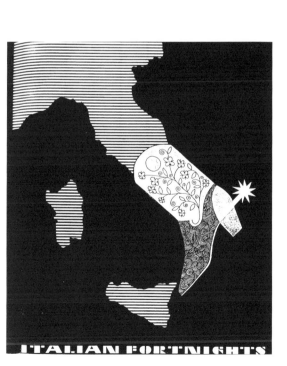

Italy "wearing" a Texan boot, advertisement

for Neiman Marcus, Dallas, Texas, 1960s

considerable contempt. Here are some excerpts from George F. Babbitt's address to the Zenith Real Estate Board, a classic of boosterism: "In other countries, art and literature are left to a lot of shabby bums living in attics and feeding on booze and spaghetti, but in America the successful writer or picture-painter is indistinguishable from any other decent business man... Here's the new generation of Americans: fellows with hair on their chests and smiles in their eyes and adding-machines in their offices... Some time I hope folks will quit handing all the credit to a lot of moth-eaten, mildewed, out-of-date, old, European dumps... Believe me, the world has fallen too long for these worn-out countries that aren't producing anything but boot-blacks and scenery and booze..." This is utilitarian Tayloristic puritanism—to quote Henry Louis Mencken: "The haunting fear that someone, somewhere, may be happy."

If ever there was a straw man, it is Babbitt, and clearly Sinclair Lewis meant to set him up as a thoroughly ridiculous representative of Mencken's booboisie, the middle America of Warren Harding and Calvin Coolidge. It is, in fact, no accident that just as the bomb-throwing bearded revolutionary from the Old Country was scaring America, prohibition was signed into law; clearly, the respectable, abstemious, straitlaced old America was trying to legislate the chaotic habits of an unruly, poverty- stricken, Levantine new America.

Babbitt scorned Italy out of hand as a land of shameful luxury and idleness, an unsettling influence, a source of anarchy and labor unrest. Still, Babbitt's Calvinistic censure of

things Italian evidently concealed that consciousness of an inferiority that Johnson cited. In a flirtatious conversation with the local bon vivant Lucile McKelvey, Babbitt ventures:

" 'I suppose you'll be going over to Europe pretty soon again, won't you?'

" 'I'd like awfully to run over to Rome for a few weeks.'

" 'I suppose you see a lot of pictures and music and curios and everything there.'

" 'No, what I really go for is: there's a little trattoria on the Via della Scrofa where you get the best fettuccine in the world.'

" 'Oh, I— Yes. That must be nice to try that. Yes.'"

Babbitt is like a child trying to read an adult novel; a bumptious character totally unmanned by Italy, the manna of the American intelligentsia. And for those opinion leaders, Italy was always the artistic and experiential gold standard.

Thirty years after Lewis wrote *Babbitt*, as Italy rebounded in what Italians call the postwar economic miracle, it recovered its age-old popular status as the latest thing. Alan Moorehead, in the April 1955 issue of *Holiday*, in an article headlined "Her Golden Hour," put it nicely: "In the past several years a vogue for everything Italian has sprung up in the outside world; for Italian movies and fashions, food and textiles and manufactured articles, even for the Italian way of life. Upon tourists in particular, who stream into the country in unbelievable numbers from early spring until late September, the country seems to have exerted a curious fascination, a kind of hunger for escape—not so much a geographic escape as an escape into time, into the past."

Italy, in fact, holds a very special place in the formation of the postwar American popular subconscious. As Hollywood-on-the-Tiber, Rome became one of the very few ancillary Hollywoods (with New York City, and, say, Monument Valley). Italy's role in American movies is treated elsewhere in this book; suffice it to say that the Italian icon is a blend of celluloid and spaghetti.

All of the founding fathers and mothers of the modern, virtual, post-privacy, nontraditional zeitgeist—from Ernest Hemingway to Jack Kerouac and Allen Ginsberg and Gregory Corso, from Orson Welles to Gore Vidal to Patricia Highsmith, from Truman Capote to David Bowie—staked a claim to Italy. Clare Boothe Luce—actress, playwright, society climber, friend of Frida Kahlo (among others), congresswoman from Connecticut, wife of Henry Luce, publisher of *Time*, *Life*, and *Fortune*—actually served as American ambassador to Italy from 1953 to 1956.

All of these founding figures in the creation of a postmodern culture presided at the birth of a glamorous, mediagenic idea of Italy. And Italy developed that exquisitely mediagenic image at a very good time, with the sweeping dematerialization of business and, indeed, of economics. Italy itself is old, very old, but in a very real sense the icon of Italy developed after World War II, making it no older than, say, the icon of Las Vegas. And Las Vegas is cited advisedly. One of the latest structures to grace the cement and neon amid the yucca flats that are Las Vegas will be called Venezia—an astonishingly odd evocation of a city built on water in a city built on sand.

But both Las Vegas and Venice are cities built on trade and on a well-planned commerce in images and luxurious experience. The image of Las Vegas was long that of Egyptian sands, sphinxes, and pyramids, but also—perhaps segueing from Cleopatra—the ancient Rome of Caesar's Palace. Ionian pillars beside swimming pools: the icon of Italy is somehow intrinsically bound up with Las Vegas, the great American dream palace, founded by a couple of Jewish mobsters and their Italian backers.

As Michael Herr makes clear in *The Big Room*, Italians and Jews had much to do with the creation of the image of Las Vegas—with this subversive, luxuriant, vibrant, tawdry, anti-Calvinist transmogrification of various, borrowed commonplaces of the American culture of luxury. Rat Pack and Godfather, show business and shady dealings: Las Vegas has a decidedly non-WASP, even Levantine, image. Jimmy Durante "played to probably the smallest audience of his career" the night after Christmas in 1946 at the opening of the Flamingo: "Most likely he agreed to make the benediction as a favor to Ben Siegel." Siegel, Lansky, Luciano, Sinatra, Martin and Lewis and Bennett... Las Vegas is a swarthy, ardent, imaginative suitor to the great American farm girl. Versace inevitably meets Liberace.

In the victorious, aggressive America of the 1950s, the ancient Roman motif of Las Vegas stood for something else: colonization. In a sense the Latins have come around again, full circle: the oldest imperialist power on earth colonizing the newest one—a cultural and economic colonization, granted. In fact, short of Assyrian winged bulls, Las Vegas features the styles of the great empires: the pyramids, Rome, now Venice, and even Napoleonic Paris, and—not far away, on Lake Havasu— even the genuine, rebuilt London Bridge.

In a sense, it is not unlike the relationship of ancient Greece with its military conqueror, Rome. A people with an older, more sophisticated culture, the Greeks simply tantalized the relatively countrified Latin occupiers with their art and music and books and style until it was socially unacceptable not to be able to read Homer in the original. Horace said "Greece ... enslaved ... made a slave of her rough conqueror," and in the same cunning fashion, Italy has become the last European nation to colonize the American continent.

Americans are behaving like a colonized nation—parroting fashionable Italian, chattering about espresso and Tuscany and latté and turkey piccata. The males of America, recognizing a good thing, adopt the Italian cultural style as best they are able. This is nothing new: two hundred years ago English dandies who affected Continental mannerisms and clothes were known, somewhat derisively, as Macaroni.

Thus, perhaps, Italy is teaching America something of its ancient, fatalistic approach to world politics. To quote from Joseph Heller's *Catch 22*: "You put so much stock in winning wars ... The real trick lies in losing wars, and in knowing which wars can be lost. Italy has been losing wars for centuries, and just see how splendidly we've done nonetheless." In the give-and-take, the incessant obsessive flirtation that links Italy and America, there are, in the final analysis, two elements in play. One is the immense romantic credibility and popularity of Italy. E. M. Forster wrote in *Room with a View*: "The traveller who has gone to Italy to study the tactile values of Giotto, or the corruption of the Papacy, may return remembering nothing but the blue sky and the men and women under it." Italy, in short, as earthly paradise. The other is the immense profitability of the trade. Versace and Armani are to Italy in the 1990s what the Beatles were to Britain in the 1960s. The Beatles were knighted not for their manners or birth but for the records they sold.

Armani, Versace, Krizia, and the whole Olympus of Italian fashion cannot be knighted; there is no queen of Italy to knight them. If television is king, however, surely Italian fashion designers have been ennobled in some lasting way in the esteem of their countrymen. Only the Pope can boast the same amount of airtime as that given fashion on the Italian airwaves.

The Italian icon is a romantic icon because it is immensely rewarding for it to be so. With apologies to Gina Lollobrigida, as Anita Loos wrote in *Gentlemen Prefer Blondes*, "So I really think that American gentlemen are the best after all, because kissing your hand may make you feel very, very good, but a diamond and safire bracelet lasts forever."

Reproduction of Michelangelo's David

at Caesar's Palace, Las Vegas, Nevada.

(Grazia Neri)

Sentimental Design

Paola Antonelli

Every country has its own international design icons for export purposes, appropriated by international popular favor and elevated to monument status. Design is another clever way Italians have found to export their foot-loose and fancy-free winning image. But Italians export more than the perfect objects that become legends most.

In fact, Italians produce beautifully imperfect objects that look great, work well, are impeccably manufactured, and yet express vulnerability. They are as directly communicative as romantic novels in that they take a shortcut to the soul of the international public. To name a few of the most successful: the Vespa of 1945, the Valentine typewriter of 1968, the Ferrari (the model does not really matter, so long as the car is flaming red), Venetian glass of the 1950s, the Bialetti coffeemaker of 1930, Cinelli racing bicycles,

the postmodern follies furniture of the 1980s, and even Madonna, if one can be allowed this double stretching both of the term "Italian product" and of "design." All these items exude the romance and passion many other countries appear to need an injection of, and Italians seem the only ones that can provide it, at least in design. Italian design is successful because of matters of global balance. A meeting of Ferrari collectors happens every year in the United States on Rodeo Drive in Los Angeles, and it is an extraordinary event. The American Ferrari aficionados swim in a sea of Ferrari red, their monuments all neatly lined up for everybody else to envy. They reach for each other to exchange war-and-love stories. In Anglo-Saxon countries, and in the United States in particular, Italian icons are surrounded by an aura of slight trans-

106

Bialetti Moka Express coffeemaker

Opposite:

Abarth Monotipo, built by Gruppo
Stola, Italian builder of models and
prototypes for major automotive
manufacturers, 1998

Cisitalia Berlinetta 202, 1947
Design by Pininfarina.
Exhibited in 1951 for the exhibition
"Eight Automobiles," curated by
Arthur Drexler at the Museum
of Modern Art in New York
and immediately acquired for
the museum's permanent collection, this automobile represents
a turning point in the image of Italy
as a nation with credibility in the
field of industrial manufacturing
in the postwar period.

Opposite:

Abarth Bialbero 750 cc.,

speed testing for the

world record for ten thousand miles,

Monza race track, 1960

(Publifoto Olympia)

gression, by the knowledge of Italians' seem-ingly exaggerated comfort with sex, as dis-played on the covers of political weeklies and in public ads for soaps, cars, and washing machines all over the country. They allow American lovers a legitimate excess. Italians can make anything sentimental, even a type-writer, not to mention a car, and for these reasons and others, Italian icons generate an immoderate passion. Italians set the grounds for appreciation by being slightly amoral, polit-ically and economically insecure (and there-fore not threatening), and then fun-loving and, after all, enviable. As a matter of fact, many of the Italian design icons that are unanimously loved around the world belong to the 1950s, when Italy was at its most vulnerable to outside influence.

One of the secrets of Italian icon designers is their capacity to fully express their time by endowing the objects with per-sonality and making them become almost co-characters in a movie scene. Each design evokes an Italian spectacle that makes it even

more desirable. Sophia Loren sits sideways on a Vespa, wearing spike heels and a scarf to keep her hair in place—the 1950s; exasper-atedly elegant, Vergottini-cut and optical-clad waifs sit nonchalantly on Blow chairs in a shiny plastic landscape—the 1960s; at the same time, Ettore Sottsass, everybody's beloved, types love letters with two fingers on the passion-red Valentine by the light of a candle; leftist intellectuals, elegantly negli-gent, rest their revolutionary brains on Sacco chairs—the 1970s; Gordon Gekko smokes his cigar under the cold light of a Tizio lamp, its profile as high-tech as his heart—the 1980s. When one appropriates an object made in Italy, be it a chair, a suit, or a Gaggia cof-feemaker, one buys into a whole image that makes one's statement not only stylistic but also visual and evocative.

Outstanding Italian design has by these means become a legend. Its first romantic construct is the recounting of how it was born. In the early 1950s, ingenious architects without jobs fortuitously met enlightened

industrial manufacturers in search of prod-ucts and inventive engineers in search of experiments. It was a triple coup de foudre. Some background history is needed: in the nineteenth century, the earthquake of the industrial revolution had separated good design from intense industrial manufacturing. In the United Kingdom, the moralist Arts and Crafts movement and its leader William Morris had drawn an ideal and somewhat biased demarcation line for everybody's future use. On one side of the line, the righ-teous side, sat the craftsman, independent maker of ideas and enlightened master of beauty and honesty toward nature. On the other side was the industrial manufacturer, mere actuator of the evil and the ugly, manip-ulator of materials against their own nature. Yet the best of design proved always to be generated in the intermediate stations. Design being, after all, a search for a perfect balance between means (the available mate-rials and techniques) and goals (for example a superlight chair, a low-cost steel floor lamp,

Toio floor lamp, 1962

Design by Achille and Pier Giacomo

Castiglioni

an affordable sportscar), when hands-on techniques were extensively substituted by industrial technologies, the ethical equation could, and often did, remain intact.

Italians could not, because of their own nature, buy into this Manichaean machination and provided many of the exceptions that upset the rule. The best examples of Italian design products reflect a tight collaboration and deep spiritual affinity between designer and manufacturer, which has given and is still giving designers from Italy and from all over the world exceptional psychological and technical support for wide experimentation with materials and technologies. Since the 1930s, good and evil were transcended in design by means of a special collaborative formula that was based on shared technical knowledge and dreams. Before World War II, this fortunate attitude presented itself in some isolated pockets, from the food industry—the case of Campari is symbolic—to the mechanical industry, with the example of the Olivetti enterprise and its outstanding chieftain, Adriano. Olivetti, a typewriter manufacturer whose company was founded in 1908 by his father, Camillo, was able to create a design heaven and a strong corporate image by hiring the best designers for the company's products; the best artists, from painters to poets, for its advertising campaigns; and the best architects for the company's buildings. Above and beyond all the immediate company interests, Adriano also made the company into a patron of the arts of the past and present. Olivetti produced at least two typewriters that became Italian icons, the Lettera 22 of 1950 and the Valentine of 1969. The Lettera 22 was designed by Marcello Nizzoli, who since

1940 had successfully attempted to endow machinery with organic sensuality.

After World War II enlightenment trickled down to the furniture and domestic-appliances industry, transforming many preexisting companies that relied not only on big contract commissions but also on trite imitations of eclectic styles in pioneers of design (such as Cassina), and shaping the destinies of the newborn companies. At that time, old and new, small and midsize companies crossed paths with many talented architects looking at industrial design in search for a concretization of their ideas. Franco Albini, Achille and Pier Giacomo Castiglioni, Carlo Scarpa, and Marco Zanuso, to name just a few, though design geniuses, could not possibly have achieved their success without the peculiar receptiveness of the industry, based especially in northern Italy, particularly in the region north of Milan and in Veneto, and in pockets in central Italy. There, the many family-based, open-minded companies reacted positively both to the refined taste of architects and to the technological innovations, becoming bigger without ever losing the flexibility that allowed architects hands-on experimentation. Other companies were created from scratch on the same industrial-craftsmanship cultural attitude, some based on new technologies, like Kartell, founded in 1949 by engineer Giulio Castelli to exploit the invention of polypropylene. Others were founded by designers and architects who wanted to produce their custom furniture in more than one piece. Italian companies of this kind, some from the 1940s and 1950s and some established more recently on the same model, have been able to maintain their experimental verve and, in a moment of shortage

Aprilia RSV Mille motorcycle,

1998

From racing victory

emerges a new cult bike.

of great Italian designers, are still keeping the Italian design flag flying high by attracting the best designers from all over the world. Olivetti's renaissance company needs to be remembered when looking at the Italian image-making companies of today. In more recent times, some companies, like Alessi, have learned from fashion to focus on the image as the export design icon, stronger than any single well-designed and well-manufactured product. The Alessi company was founded in 1921 by Giovanni Alessi Anghini as a plate-turning workshop. It has since become one of the most recognizable brands for good design worldwide and has spread from the production of steel housewares to virtually any material and category of domestic objects and small furnishings. Not unlike Olivetti, Alberto Alessi, the public face of the company, has imposed himself as a mentor for great designers of all ages. In the

Italjet Velocifero, 1993

Design by Centro Stile Italjet

The first scooter with an aluminum body,

the founder of the "neo-retrodesign" line.

spirit of the 1990s, though, Alessi has also marketed the designers' images. Not unlike Olivetti, Alessi successfully publishes books, produces limited art series, and commissions architectural projects. While the company still relies on the evergreen classical steelwares that are ubiquitous in Italian homes and bars—from sugar bowls to pots and pans and salt and pepper shakers—it also carefully planned a massive diversification of production. Under all these labels one can find such sub-icons as Philippe Starck's mean citrus squeezer, Michael Graves's chirping kettle, Richard Sapper's coffeepot, and Robert Venturi's penis-shaped stove lighter, to mention just a few. Alessi truly is the postmodern Olivetti.

This level of appreciation of Italian design is nonetheless quite elitist and more common in Europe, especially in Great Britain, where Italian design milestones such as the Vespa and the Lambretta truly became significant in popular culture. Even though Alessi and a few other companies are trying a commercial expansion in foreign countries, much of the praised Italian industrial and furniture design remains outside of the real international market, or levitates above it with a nonchalant air of superiority. Vehicles and lighting fixtures are often not manufactured to match international standards outside of Europe. The production is not boosted to reach competitive retail prices. Most iconic cars, furniture, tabletop objects, and appliances are either difficult to maintain or just too expensive because of the size of the companies, the investment in research, and the inadequate distribution. Popular international outreach does not seem to be most Italian manufacturers' worry or responsibility. The Italian legend is made of a series of dream objects, most of which remain among people's desires and can never really penetrate their daily lives.

Nonetheless, there exists an Italian design field that proves to be really successful at all cultural levels and in all countries: food. Food is the most universal stereotype of Italian design, for good and for bad. In the mid-1990s, the office of Mayor Rudolph Giuliani in New York mailed an invitation

Illy X1espresso maker, 1996

Design by Luca Trazzi

The design was inspired

by the dashboard of the first Fiat 500

to an Italian celebration that was illustrated with a cut salami and a flask of wine—no mandolin—and not with an Armani suit or a Vespa. Pasta, amaretti, baci, pizza, Galliano, and Campari are all the product of design efforts, efforts that for the most part remain subliminal. They are not acknowledged by the public as intellectual intentions, and are therefore even more powerful. Food, pasta for example, is the basic anonymous design, the effective point at which high elaboration meets popular culture.

All in all, Italians have been the best at designing evocative symbols. And nowadays, even in a country as disorganized in its corporate image communication as Italy, the best examples of furniture and industrial design managed to team up with the food and fashion industry to project a national image of outstanding manufacture and continuous design quality, the good design of a nation.

Classic pieces of
Italian industrial design:

Black ST 201 television made
of methacrylate, 1969
Design by Marco Zanuso and
Richard Sapper, Brionvega

Ariante personal fan, 1974
Design by Marco Zanuso,
Vortice

Tizio lamp made of
aluminum and resin, 1972
Design by Richard Sapper,
Artemide.

("Collezione per un Modello di Museo
del Disegno Industriale Italiano")

Songs with Wings

Carlo Antonelli

"Rome with Love" album cover

Photograph by Andrea Pol

Opposite:

Poster for the movie

"Nel Blu Dipinto di Blu—Volare,"

directed by Piero Tellini, 1959

(Farabolafoto)

I believe that to discuss the spread of Italian music throughout the world, we should broaden our point of view (instead of reviewing an admittedly extensive list of Italian popular songs that have conquered the world with their distinctive and at times heartbreaking sentimental approach; instead of conducting an analysis, however learned, of what actually distinguishes Italian music from all other kinds of music in the world) and attempt to consider the paltry and reductive nature of a definition of music bound up with a single nation, at least if we are talking about the most popular recordings of the twentieth century.

Music, Jacques Attali once said, has always been a forerunner and bellwether of the forms of exchange in the economy of the future. It is an immaterial merchandise that travels on exceedingly light media (the human breath, paper, pieces of wax or vinyl, compact discs, electronic files) and is subject, more than most other forms of merchandise, to methods of diffusion that are difficult to control, liable to unhindered reproduction. The legal sanctions first established more than a century ago (societies of

authors and composers, and copyright laws in general) have been inadequate to hinder the complicated and bizarre paths taken by melodies. Songs are strange objects, things that we cannot touch but that have exceedingly long legs. They pass from mouth to mouth, on foot (whistled as we walk down the street), by ship (sung by all the passengers to help overcome fear of the deep), aboard tanks (in order to establish a sense of togetherness in the face of the dangers of war), and on airplanes, always helping to link our hearts—at least—to the places we live and come from, often very distant or even entirely imaginary. Songs are strange creations, things that in theory belong to someone (which is why they are registered, with first and last names of the supposed composer, in the various societies of composers, artists, and performers); but, in fact, once you hear a song being hummed by someone in a bar, that song becomes another song, with a different title, similar to the original song only here and there, and so a new song, strangely original. It is still possible to establish the ownership of and rights to an entire song;

Album covers from the 1950s

Italian music in an export version.

it is much harder to do so with little bits of that song (as samplers know very well). A strange business, is it not? This has been the situation for at least a hundred years, long before software, the Internet, the digital copy that is indistinguishable from the original.

War in the Ears

Music is ubiquitous in the twentieth century. "Radio did not change music," wrote Eric J. Hobsbawm in *The Age of Extremes*, "but the role of music in contemporary life, not excluding its role as aural wallpaper for everyday living, is inconceivable without it." The gramophone, already widespread, had begun to fill the air with sound. The aesthetic and economic warfare, then, that is being waged in our ears is a rich one, a war that was won—in terms of popular music—by the Americans, save for a few theaters of war that met with defeat by the turn of the twentieth century. "No other national or regional model established itself globally," Hobsbawm goes on to point out, "though some had substantial regional influence (for instance, Egyptian music within the Islamic world) and an occasional exotic touch entered global commercial popular culture from time to time, as in the Caribbean and Latin American components of dance music." The music of the twentieth century, whether classical or popular, stands out for its marked openness to the new, the manifold, sounds never before heard, rejected distant marginal sounds, accompanied by an attitude that contains in itself the concept of total control of the unknown, of the unsettling.

There is, in short, a close relationship between economic and aesthetic matters. The purchase and sale of sound equipment provokes clashes between dominant cultures and subalternate ones. The Italian popular song has cheerfully withstood body blows from one and all: the French music of the Second Empire and the Belle Epoque, the tango, the Charleston, the fox-trot, swing music, light jazz, the all-American musical, and South American rhythms—which is to

say nothing at all of rock and roll. Rock and roll has become the lingua franca of youth culture in the second half of the twentieth century, a genre (with economic repercussions, let us be perfectly clear; we should have no illusions that music is immaterial) that pioneered the future worldwide spread of brand names. Rock and roll allowed the young people of the 1960s all over the world to acquire an immediate identity; the same was true for Italy, where the cover song—an Italian version of a popular non-Italian hit, with all its exotic and cinematic allure—became a formidable tool of musical colonization and hybridization (from the Middle Eastern experiments of Renato Carosone to the original gangster ballads of Fred Buscaglione; from the belters Mina and Celentano to Gianni Morandi and Rita Pavone; from the summertime twist of Edoardo Vianello all the way to the beat explosion of groups such as Equipe 84, Camaleonti, Dik Dik, Pooh, New Trolls, Ribelli, Corvi, and Giganti). The idea of purchasing identity in a box or a can underlies even the spread of ethnic music around the world, including Italian music (this phenomenon is a forerunner of the spread of global culture now underway). There emerged therefore—through the spread of music (but we could say the same thing about food and cooking)—over the course of the entire century, strange fascinations, impossible hybrids, unprecedented and noteworthy grafts. If someone wants an exotic Italian touch in music, what Italy will that person purchase?

Genuine and Artificial: Neapolitan Canzone and Opera

Of course, no one wants the local, pidgin versions of songs and styles that developed elsewhere, and certainly no one is interested in the one genuine innovation, the pop use of noise developed by the futurists. What people want from Italy is something that cannot be found anywhere else: high opera and Neapolitan music—with apologies to Gramsci—Italy's serious contributions to global pop culture. As is always the

case, it takes foreign visitors to render embarrassing the absurdities and oddities of home, or even to render visible the features of home itself. The leading distributor of Neapolitan music at the beginning of the twentieth century was a German publisher, Polyphon Musikverleger of Leipzig. There were notable emigrants (for instance, Luigi Denza, who composed songs such as "Funiculì Funiculà" and who taught bel canto at the Royal Academy of Music in London at the end of the nineteenth century). For about a century, right up to the end of the 1930s, Naples and its gulf were the most frequently sung-about places on earth (everyone knows the songs, from "Santa Lucia" to "'O paese d'o sole" to "'O sole mio") by virtue of a flourishing of music that has no rivals in history, like New Orleans for ragtime jazz, Vienna for the waltz, and Buenos Aires for the tango. Quite slowly, via the ships loaded with Italians that moored at Ellis Island after the usual thirty-day journey, this all moved to New York.

In 1883, even before the great Italian immigration of the turn of the century, the Metropolitan Opera House was inaugurated. It was managed from 1908 to 1935 by Giulio Gatti-Casazza, who brought Toscanini and Caruso to America. Italian immigrants throughout the world were to light the fuse (the famous melody "Core ingrato" was written for Caruso by two Italian Americans), and also to create such masterpieces of syncretism as "Chist'è New York," "L'americana 'e Napule," "E canfuncelle d'America" and so on, ranging from "Santa Lucia luntana" to "Core furastiero" to the heartrending "'O paese d'o sole"—this last song entirely focused on the yearning for a distant home, an emigrant's nostalgia, too extreme to be true, which marked forever the idea of Italian musical expression.

Is it still possible to think—as did Rousseau and the French Encyclopedists, who clearly preferred the music of Italy to their own—that Italian musicality continues to stand out for its melodiousness, freshness, and natural sound? The characteristic of Italian opera—and of opera in general—that is most widely appreciated is certainly not spontaneity but rather the totally artificial nature of the formula, the absolutely original and at the same time false confluence of elements of pathos with quaint and touching sources, often exotic in the most two-dimensional fashion (to cite just one example, an apparent forerunner of the movies or television, Puccini's *La Fanciulla del West*). Opera, for that matter, consists of precisely this transition, according to the analysis of Giovanni Macchia: the transition from the sincerity of nature to a gorgeous artifice, the need to discover one's own vital awareness within the context of a denunciation of a radical crisis, a declaration of a shattered order, a lost rhythm, and dispersed unity. This is what the international public values in Italian music and wants to purchase—to some extent out of admiration, to an equal extent out of a sense of playfulness—both ingenuity and genuineness: the rascally power of sentiment, an absolute lack of shame or modesty, an artificial horror at pain, however minimal. Nothing could seem more exotic to the harsh puritan sensibility. The exaggeration of the pathos makes the source of the suffering improbable, reducing it in importance, shrinking it to a pure exercise in rhetoric.

Sinatra and Presley (with a cover version of "'O sole mio"—"It's Now or Never") were to find themselves obliged to make use of the ultimate weapon—the great melody of Italy and Naples—in order to attain the furthest spheres of masculine sentimentality. The careful use, finally, of the Neapolitan tradition and opera arias mixed with the great American pop hits found in the excellent sound tracks of movies by Scorsese (from *Mean Streets* to *Goodfellas*) and in the three parts of Coppola's *Godfather* contributed to the consolidation of a legend of a certain weird sentimentality in the Italian race. It was this specific component, at once theatrical and athletic, of Italian music that led to the worldwide triumph of Italian singers during the course of the twentieth century.

Souvenirs of Italy: Travelers and Tourists

Is it possible to separate the myth of Enrico Caruso from the fact that he was one of the first—if not the very first—hero of recorded music? Caruso's career began in 1897 at the Teatro Lirico in Milan, followed by the triumphs of Monte Carlo, Paris, London, Saint Petersburg, Buenos Aires, and New York, where he debuted at the Metropolitan in 1903 in *Rigoletto*; until 1920 he remained the beloved superstar of the Met and the American listening public. He traveled everywhere, and everywhere he went, his records arrived before him, as if to prepare the way. He was the first great immaterial star of recorded song (with apologies to the supposed lack of artifice of the Italian canzone). In his wake, practically in the same concert halls

Mina, 1960s

Italian pop music

(Grazia Neri)

scattered across the face of the world, came Beniamino Gigli and Tito Schipa. Together they were an exalted and untouchable trinity, enshrined in the hearts of Italy's emigrants: they posed for photographs wearing fur coats purchased in Russia and diamond rings nearly the size of the Ritz, aboard their yachts wearing sailor caps. Then came Luciano Tajoli, the second great global star of Italian melody (he recorded five hundred songs for Columbia Records): he filled the theaters in Buenos Aires and on Broadway; he was mobbed in Australia; in Toronto in 1954, he wore a fur coat and rode down the street in a motorcade, like a president; he was accorded a triumphal reception in Caracas; in 1965, during a memorable tour in Japan, he recorded "Tsujoku" ("Abbracciami Forte," or "Hold Me Tight") and sold out at the Eagle's Nest at the Hilton in Hong Kong with a series of hits (" 'O sole mio," "Santa Lucia," "Abbracciami forte," and "L'Aldilà," co-authored with Mogol, which by 1961 had made the rounds of piano lounges, Las Vegas first and foremost among them). Though suffering from polio, he was everywhere. Then—again during the 1950s and the 1960s—came Claudio Villa, the tenor/nontenor, with "Vecchia Roma" and "Luna Rossa" and the incredible "Granada," all songs loved by Pasolini, on a triumphal tour around the world (including Moscow, by now a regular stop on the itinerary, where Villa was photographed wearing a bearskin hat). And even Renato Carosone toured like a maniac, trotting around the globe—at the end of the 1950s, he was in Spain, and then Paris, Athens, New York, Toronto, London, Caracas, Buenos Aires, Havana, Rio, and São Paulo.

Looming over all others was the uncommon genius of Domenico Modugno. "His melodic inventivity contained a confluence of every sort of popular detritus from the entire Mediterranean basin," wrote Massimo Mila about Modugno's early years. "Rossini went arm-in-arm with Duke Ellington. Modugno was the only royal flush that Italian music could claim in the face of the triumphs of the French 'chanson' or

Adriano Celentano and Claudia Mori,

winners of the Festival di Sanremo, 1970

(Publifoto Olympia)

the blues created by black Americans." And so it was: at the Festival di Sanremo in 1958, accompanied by Maestro Semprini, Modugno, his arms spread wide, triumphed with "Nel Blu Dipinto di Blu"—or "Volare," as everyone was to call it from then on, selling millions of records everywhere. And where the records went, Modugno himself soon followed.

Nearly thirty years earlier, another traveling songbird, Odoardo Spadaro, wrote—at the end of the 1930s, in Montevideo, after a successful tour in Paris and Berlin—"Porti un Bacione a Firenze," or, literally, "Send a Big Kiss to Florence": in time, this concept was to become a recurrent and popular theme of foreign tourism in Italy, along with the seemingly endless production of nostalgic light melodies linked to classic vacation spots of the 1950s. In 1956, ten million tourists visited Italy: popular music soon teemed with invitations to remember Rimini, to meet again in Rapallo, to bid each other a fond "auf Wiedersehen" at Diano Marina, to stroll together at least for a night in Viareggio, to spend long summers in Taormina, and to gaze fondly up at the moon over Capri. "I Found My Love in Portofino," by Buscaglione, was one, as was the spectacular "I Sing Amore," by Nicola Arigliano (on the other side of the Atlantic Ocean, during the same period, Dean Martin provided a musical response with his astonishing "That's Amore"). And looming high above all others was "Souvenir d'Italie," which made its debut in 1956 in the version sung by the Indian vocalist Amru Sari, with verses in the Neapolitan dialect and a refrain in French.

Italians/Non-Italians: Strange Modern Identities

All the same, melodic viruses aside (we shall not even attempt to emphasize the point that Italian melodies still influence and dominate the Latin regions of the world, traditionally the homeland of world rhythm), the unjustified force of these men who barrel at full speed into the barriers of their own voices lies at the foundation of the unparalleled success of Luciano

Pavarotti and Andrea Bocelli—and it is no accident that these are more international than local phenomena. Italian music at the end of the twentieth century is opposing the anonymity of the modern—in what is practically a quantum leap backward to grand opera, now triumphing around the world—with powerful, even titanic individuals, distinctive, not subject to standardization, unique because they are not afraid of expressing embarrassingly sentimental concepts: this is true of the lover boy Eros Ramazzotti and of the girl next door, sweet but strong as a rock—Laura Pausini. Once again, the predominance of the emotional side and a powerful vocal quality overwhelm all the rest, as if these were survivors of the standardized horrors of modernity. This is what the mass audiences of the twentieth century desire from Italian music, and this is in part restored, with a careful construction—at the drawing board—of soluble Italianities, ready to be consumed.

But there is a new wave of musical consumers, with different, more sophisticated and exclusive tastes, yearning for revivals—no longer of ethnic culture but rather bound up with the local versions of the gigantic and sweeping process of modernization that roared like a tornado through every nation in the 1950s and 1960s (note the essay by Peppino Ortoleva in this book). Cultural studies departments do research into Pasolini and Antonioni as serious components of an original emotional and aesthetic definition of (post)modernity; in much the same manner the B movie industry—indeed the Z movie industry—of those years has been borrowed for use in a practically endless musical game, based on a recovery of the strange artificial Italian beat of the 1960s and 1970s (not to mention the revival of Italy's classically inspired progressive rock, underway in Japan for some time now: from Morricone and Ortolani to Piccioni and Umiliani, and on and on in an infinite series of clones

of these artists, other composers of sound tracks for dirty movies). The recycling of Italy's strange modern music is still in its earliest stage and it is no accident that this is an international phenomenon much more than a domestic one. There is no other reasonable explanation—without referring to Hollywood on the Tiber, in the Cinecittà of those years—for a group of sophisticated Japanese groove makers who decided to call their own label Trattoria (with one chart-busting star, Kahimi Karie, who in 1995 launched an unforgettable microhit "Una Giapponese a Roma" —"A Japanese Woman in Rome"—a song that opens with a car horn honking, taken from the sound track of the Dino Risi movie *Il sorpasso*). For that matter, what does the name of the girl group Cibo Matto suggest? It is interesting to think that new generations are no longer so insistent on acquiring portable, two-dimensional identities (and among them I would also list the refined catalogues of world music from the 1980s) of the I-buy-you-because-you-are-yourself variety but rather are focused on the opposite, the I-buy-you-because-you-are-trying-not-to-be-yourself-(and-you-are-unsuccessful) types, the laughable failures of assimilation to the aesthetic canons of large-scale capital. The successful efforts, on the other hand, include the third musical export genre par excellence of the past twenty years: Italian spaghetti dance music.

This genre originated in small studios in Bologna, with the experimentation of Mauro Malavasi (who developed the song "Changes" sung by Luther Vandross) and Celso Valli, from Savage to Dan Harrow in the 1980s, all the way up to the incredible boom of Italian house music, by such groups as Black Box, 49ers, Tipical, Cappella, Corona, Datura, and company in the early 1990s. "It's incredible: it's in such poor taste that it's thrilling," commented the British DJs of this period. Italian dance music takes the impersonal design of the dance floor to its logical extreme: it reduces soul to a hysterical stutter and bodies to phantoms, deprives human voices of their subjects, uses anonymous ghostwriters and pseudonyms in place of composers and artists, trots out improbable English names. It was an instant hit. Deep down, the characteristics remained unchanged: passionate exag-

geration, a two-dimensional perception and feeling of existence, a gaiety that is idiotic and insincere. Italian dance music took in millions over a period of five years, thanks in part to its video-game velocity in making changes, much faster than the multinationals in the same market. Italian pop music, for that matter, is full of Italians/non-Italians: from Bella Otero to the chanteuses Yvonne de Fleuril and Gina de Chamery of the tabarins (or nightclubs) and the caffè concerto of the turn of the century right up to the fake-Russian, fake-Japanese, fake-Turkish soubrettes of the revue of Macario at the end of the 1930s, and on and on—to the three little Dutch sisters of the Trio Lescano (widely believed to be "italianissime"), and the "rockers all'amatriciana," Bobby Solo and Little Tony, the hollering singer Betty Curtis, the black dancer straight out of a cartoon, Rocky Roberts, and finally reaching the present-day dance clones.

What national identity is expressed by Bocelli, the sound tracks of sexy movies from the 1960s, the cheesy piano music of Black Box, the hybrids of Asian Dub, and the great Neapolitan melodia of the Almamegretta? "The promiscuous European," wrote Nietzsche in the nineteenth century, "absolutely requires customs; history is necessary to him as a wardrobe of customs. In truth, he invariably notices that no custom really fits—he changes and changes his customs. The nineteenth century distinguishes itself by these rapid shifts and new preferences in the mascarades of styles." Only now, at the turn of the twenty-first century, are we beginning to notice, belatedly, that national styles are nothing but games —at times amusing and self-aware, more often quite ingenuous—involving strategies of rhetoric in the context of a largely general and solidly immaterial economic system.

Below: Eros Ramazzotti

Photograph by Franco Origlia

(Grazia Neri)

Above: Claudio Villa at the

Festival di Sanremo, 1967

(Publifoto Olympia)

Celluloid Italians

Pierre Sorlin

Is there a "film Italian"? An Italian actor or actress playing a role in an Italian movie, in Italy, is not Italian; he or she is just a character, with no particular notation of nationality. But they become Italian when, in a non-Italian movie, they are called upon to depict the specific traits of Italianness. These characters, clearly artificial, are products, on the one hand, of stereotypes, conventional and recurrent models of behavior, and, on the other hand, of the varying relations that non-Italians have with Italy. In classic Hollywood films, from the 1930s to the 1960s, an Italian is an immigrant who has trouble fitting into American society; in later decades, as Asians and Chicanos arrived en masse in the United States, the Italian makes it and fits in—perhaps fitting in just a bit too well: this is the entire development of cinema, from *Little Caesar* to *Scarface* and *The Godfather*.

The titles just mentioned might lead us to think that the Italian on screen will be a gangster or an outlaw. It is true that in detective pictures or film noir, about 20 percent of the criminals are Italian—a share outnumbered only by the share of Irish criminals. The entire matter becomes more complex to the degree that—as well as being criminals—film Italians are also victims and policemen. In American movies, especially, there is a clear link between the underworld and Italianness, but a considerable percentage of the film Italians, rather than being involved in criminal activities, are the victims of organized crime. And, even before television's Lieutenant Colombo, there were film Italians who were fighting on the right side of the law.

Aside from crime and its indirect effects, just how are Italians seen in Hollywood movies? Well, they are Catholic, they have a crucifix hanging on the wall at home, but on screen, religion is less important for Italians than it is for the Irish. The Italians certainly aren't pioneer stock; unlike the Irish or the Chicanos, they do not take part in the winning of the West, and they are virtually

Ray Liotta, Robert De Niro,
Paul Sorvino, and Joe Pesci
in Goodfellas, directed by
Martin Scorsese, 1990

(Farabolafoto)

Paul Muni in Scarface,

directed by Howard Hawks, 1932

(Farabolafoto)

never seen in Westerns. They live in the city, they live among themselves, in their own neighborhoods, and they form an exceedingly close-knit community, based primarily on family.

In the movie *Cry of the City*, Lieutenant Candella tries to set the Sicilian bandit Martin Rome back on the straight and narrow; when he realizes that the bandit is simply beyond redemption, he goes after him mercilessly because —as he explains to Rome—crime dishonors all of the inhabitants of Little Italy. Ideology condemns a man whom he has not known and seen socially since childhood; the Italian police lieutenant does not hesitate to incarcerate a buddy who has fallen into evil ways. This solidity of community and moral ties allows Italians to get by in an unfavorable environment.

Dishonest and sly though he may be, Gino, the head of the Monetti family in *House of Strangers*, can count on the blind loyalty of his son, who goes to prison for seven years in his father's place. On the other hand, in *The Brothers Rico*, the fact that the eldest son has become an important businessman and has fallen out of touch with his family creates a horrible situation, culminating in the death of the younger brothers. As filmed by Hollywood, Italians are un-American.

It is difficult to translate that most American of adjectives into Italian. It does not mean "non-American"; rather, it means extraneous to the American tradition. Lieutenant Colombo is un-American because he dresses badly, he has a broken-down car, and he is not trying to get ahead in the police department. The "Colombo" series is a parody that contradicts what actually happens in the United States. Film Italians are un-American in a different way. In classic movies, the audience is amazed and amused at the sight of mothers treating adult sons and daughters like little children, or fathers wielding absolute authority over their offspring, monitoring their every move, arranging their marriages. On screen, the Italian family amused and deeply touched the moviegoing public, which places value on the individual and on personal initiative; in 1955 America gave a national standing ovation to *Marty*, a film that was moving, if not particularly good. It told the story of the life of a timid man, a butcher of Italian descent, Marty Pilletti, who at the age of thirty-five lives somewhere in the Bronx, totally subjugated by his overbearing mother; Marty becomes a real American the day he finds the courage to rebel and choose a wife that his mother cannot accept. The case of *Marty* illustrates perfectly the

prejudices of a society that considers itself tolerant but demands that everyone conform to its rules.

The tight-knit Italian family or clan didn't just make people laugh, it frightened them. The America of the 1950s was obsessed by a fear of plots, and a committee was established, under the guidance of Senator Estes Kefauver, to investigate organized crime, especially the Mafia. Americans—first during the Great Depression and again during the Cold War—tend to see the world in black and white; they believe that, with God's help, good will triumph. When Camonte, the famous Scarface, tries to take over Chicago, he is foiled by the Feds. Thirty years later, post-Vietnam America no longer believes in the ultimate triumph of justice, sees its universe as ruled by uncontrollable forces, and considers evil so powerful that, at the very best, it can only be reined in. The Mafia families in *The Godfather* go to war, and authorities are afraid to intervene; in *The Godfather, Part II* the clan that runs the money-grubbing machine of the casino takes care of justice on its own, and the police prefer to look the other way.

American mythology of the 1980s put policemen and gangsters on the same level; the young Italian in *The Untouchables*, who becomes a detective and fights against Al Capone, is motivated by his own poverty, and would have become a criminal if the opportunity had presented itself. "Redskins," as Native Americans were long dubbed, also formed part of the mythology of North America. Hollywood has always been fascinated with Indian customs, though portraying them in a fairly shallow manner.

Of the Italians, we almost never see tradi-

tions or ways of life. In 1974, a year after *Mean Streets*, Martin Scorsese made *Italianamerican*, a short documentary that is both likable and well made. He films his parents, conveying the image of a family that is not oppressive but—while remaining perfectly Americanized—that preserves a powerful bond with its past. The lesson on the art of making meatballs imparted by the mother is an excellent piece of cinema. How can we explain the fact that this rich heritage is not presented often enough in Italian-American films? In order to understand this, we must explore the way the studio system worked.

Until the 1980s, that is to say, until the development of the independents, producers would manage films in line with the purest Fordism: on an assembly line, with the entire production under a gimlet eye. A director cannot introduce surprises into the screenplay; the writers, who know nothing about the Italian community, settle for broad stereotypes. One particularly interesting aspect has to do with the choice of actors. The problem is not so much a matter of finding an Italian physiognomy but rather finding a face that is well known to the audience and capable of conveying immediately who is the good guy and who is the bad buy. The Polish-born actor Paul Muni and the Romanian-born actor Edward G. Robinson became Italian gangsters—Muni plays Capone and Robinson plays Rico Bandello—and both of them were chosen for their alien, odd look. A typical case is that of the actor Lee J. Cobb—of proper American origin—who, because of his impressively homely mug, was systematically cast as an Italian outlaw, to the point that he has played a Mafioso in a number of Italian movies, such as *Il Giorno della Civetta*,

Asia Argento, young star
of the Nuovo Cinema Italiano
and "old-fashioned" sex symbol
on the cover of Max magazine, 1998

Gina Lollobrigida, advertising

posters from the 1950s

(Fondazione Cineteca Italiana)

where he plays a Mafia boss. An actor who only wanted to wow his audience, and who cared nothing about atmosphere or behavior that might evoke everyday life in Little Italy, Paul Muni created—in *Scarface*—a perfect image of perverse, demented cruelty, caring little for the fact that his character had nothing to do with a real Italian-American.

These stereotypes were established during the classic period of cinema, and as they were shown over and over, they become well-known models, accepted by everyone. When a new generation came upon the scene in the 1960s, assimilated into American society and aware of the richness of its past—the generation that produced Scorsese and Robert De Niro, to name just two of the most famous members—it was too late to back up. Directors and actors fleshed out the view of Italians: there are scenes in *Mean Streets* that evoke the setting of Little Italy with its powerful

126

Sabrina Ferilli, "bellissima" in the
"Italic" tradition, on the cover of
Max magazine, 1998

religious tradition in a lovely portrayal of the Festival of San Gennaro, but here, as in *Casino*, the Italians remain unequivocally violent, cunning, and dangerous to everyone else.

A film Italian can never escape his destiny, and if an Italian actor gets a part in a non-Italian film, he is decadent, like Marcello Mastroianni in *Leo the Last*, or dishonest, prolix, clever, and sentimental, like Roberto Benigni in *Down by Law*. Based on established information that it then went on to exaggerate and generalize, the American film industry, seen around the world, has created—for the pleasure of its audience, an audience that did not love immigrants—a fictitious character, giving an international significance to the word "Mafia." Fortunately, the Italians—unlike the Irish, the Native Americans, and the Chicanos—were able to respond with a film industry of their own: for the rest of the world, the film Italian comes from Cinecittà, not Hollywood.

Three Euros in the Fountain

Thomas Hine

Tony Shalhoub and Stanley Tucci in Big Night,

directed by Stanley Tucci and Campbell Scott, 1996

(Farabolafoto)

I'm seventeen thousand feet above North Carolina, bound for La Guardia. Steaming on my tray table is a rectangle of airplane lasagna—layers of leathery pasta glued together with indeterminate cheese. Unfortunately, Delta Airlines has chosen to accompany this meal with the movie *Big Night*, a mouthwatering film that equates moral integrity with the determination to prepare perfect risotto.

The 1996 film, set in a New Jersey beach resort during the 1950s, concerns two brothers, recently arrived from Italy, who have opened a restaurant called Paradise. Primo, the chef, is determined to serve classic dishes without compromise. His brother, Secondo, admires Primo's artistry, but the success of Pascal's, a nearby restaurant that serves bastardized Italian-Max American cuisine—the ancestor of the lasagna before me—makes him wonder whether their Paradise can survive.

The film depends on the audience to agree that the obsessive, prickly Primo is correct, while those who flock to Pascal's, where red sauce covers all, are foolishly benighted. On the airplane, filled mainly with old people returning from winter in Florida, this premise did not work. "Why won't he serve a side of spaghetti with the entrée?" a woman in

128

Sophia Loren posing for photographers, 1954 (Grazia Neri)

the row behind me asks her husband. "I think you have a right to expect that." But most younger audiences—those who have kept pace with the changing meaning of Italy in pop culture—would probably find Primo's seriousness to be justified. They would agree that his attempt to keep a great tradition alive in a new land is worthier than the traditional American dream of wealth and success that is exemplified by Pascal's.

The contemporary audience feels it has a more accurate, more nuanced sense of Italian food and of things Italian in general. Italy is a high-value place. They've taken expensive vacations there. They know about Tizio lamps and Gianni Versace. They drink cappuccino and say ciao. In the United States, the assimilation of Italian-American culture into the mainstream has freed Italy from an immigrant image. At some mysterious moment in the 1970s, spaghetti became pasta, brands such as Gucci became popular enough to pirate, and the stereotype of the organ-grinder and his monkey were forgotten almost entirely. This change brought new American distortions of Italian culture—pear-and-goat-cheese pizza, for instance—but they were expensive and precious, not cheap and abundant, as the old stereotype had it.

Once, America was seen as a paradise for immigrants. Big Night's Paradise is a vision of Italy uncompromised by American culture. And the film's audience is willing to accept dour, difficult Primo not merely as a great cook but as a hero for giving a benighted public what it would learn to want decades later. Campbell Scott and Stanley Tucci, the writer-directors of Big Night (Tucci also plays Secondo) were shrewd in their choice of a historical moment in which to set their story. The early 1950s were a golden moment for Italian-Americans in American culture. In the moments before rock conquered all, Tony Bennett, Dean Martin, Perry Como, Vic Damone, Al Martino, Jerry Vail, Julius La Rosa, and, preeminently, Frank Sinatra ruled the radio. In Big Night, the brothers' hoped-for savior is the bandleader and novelty singer Louis Prima, who was known for doing Italian folk songs in the manner of Louis Armstrong. By comparing some of the films made during that period—ones in which Italian settings were popular—with more recent films in which the idea of Italy plays a part, it is possible to see how dramatically the idea of Italy has changed in the English-speaking world.

In Roman Holiday (1953), for example, the Italian capital serves as suitably exotic decor for the fairy-tale romance of a foreign princess, played by Audrey Hepburn, and an American journalist, played by Gregory Peck. The film has few Italian characters; their role is primarily to look the other way and allow the affair to proceed. Italy has long been seen as a place for trying things you wouldn't dare do at home—even if you're a princess.

When the sexually repressed teacher played by Katharine Hepburn in David Lean's Summertime (1955) fell into the Grand Canal, you knew that she was due for the sort of baptism into sensuality that countless English and American heroines have found in Italy. (At the time, though, there was a lot of publicity about the health risks Hepburn took when she splashed into the filthy water.) This tradition is still alive. A Room with a View (1986) demonstrated that going to Florence can induce an English girl to pick a more spirited Englishman than she might choose at home, while Enchanted April (1992) showed that Tuscany can revive your sex life. The Roman Spring of Mrs. Stone (1961) offered a sordid twist on the theme of opening yourself to life with the help of Italian men. In this Tennessee Williams story, Vivian Leigh plays a washed-up American actress who retires to Rome for a life of humiliation by an Italian gigolo, played by Warren Beatty. This film reflects a long-standing English-language literary tradition that Italians are worldly-wise, manipulatively charming, and deeply cynical. Like their land, they have seen everything.

Three Coins in the Fountain (1954) while not a very good movie, is nevertheless a very revealing one. Its story of three young American girls looking for experience and husbands in Rome followed an old Hollywood formula. The twist here—perhaps to be expected in a film with coins in its title—was the foreign exchange rate. The girls' U.S. government salary is paid in dollars, but as the most experienced of them explains to the newcomer, a mere secretary's wages add up to a princely sum in lire, allowing the young women luxuries and choices they wouldn't have in New York. A classic women's movie, it was a dream of freedom in a glamorous locale. (Filmmakers at the time were responding to a

similar set of attractions: unique locations, excellent production facilities, and low costs. These help explain Italy's popularity in American films of the period.)

With its monetary fixation, *Three Coins in the Fountain* is a sort of parable for imperialists. The natives, Italians in this case, are seen as an attractive menace—it's best to keep your distance. The Romans—even though they did once have an empire of their own—are depicted in the film as fun-loving peasants, given to driving beat-up jalopies into the countryside for joyous but irresponsible afternoons of wine, food, and song. It's all very seductive. Italians in the movies always know how to enjoy life. But heaven forbid that you should end up marrying a man who gets paid in lire!

The coins thrown in the Trevi Fountain do their work when each of the three girls finds a man. One marries her cold-fish American boss, another snags a prince, and the third does end up with an Italian, but at least he's Rossano Brazzi. Besides, you might as well throw those lire into the fountain. Italian coins aren't good for anything else.

Federico Fellini's rather different use of the same fountain in *La Dolce Vita* (1960) helped spell an end to Marshall Plan romances like those in *Three Coins in the Fountain. La Dolce Vita* won a large audience in the United States, the first Italian film to do so, and it presented an image of sophistication, decadence, and intriguing complexity that its American audience had never seen before. Moreover, Marcello Mastroianni

132

embodied age-old characteristics of the Latin lover while muting the lounge lizard overtones. Remaining quintessentially Italian, he also seemed real.

Throughout the 1960s, Italian films continued to be quite popular in the United States, and Americans depended on Italians—not Americans on location—to tell them what Italy was about. Largely, it was about sex and Sophia Loren. Italian films of the 1960s offered women with breasts even larger than those of the Hollywood films of the 1950s, and the movies in which they appeared were far sexier. Earlier, the Italian man had fulfilled the fantasies of English-speaking women. Suddenly Italy was a land of goddesses.

The commercial success of Italian cinema during the 1960s encouraged foreign filmmakers to use Italy for costume epics—like the anticlimactic Elizabeth Taylor version of *Cleopatra* (1963)—rather than for contemporary subjects. Perhaps the most intriguing bit of cultural cross-fertilization of the 1960s was the spaghetti Western, Italian interpretations of America's most typical genre. Sergio Leone's *A Fistful of Dollars* (1964) made the hitherto marginal American actor Clint Eastwood into an international star. While American Westerns often hinge on the attempt to establish moral perfection in a corrupt place—an idea that shows up in *Big Night* as well—in Leone's Italian Westerns, everyone was corrupt. In the Vietnam era, Americans were willing to admit Italian cynicism to their national epic.

The seamlessness of corruption

Vivien Leigh and Warren Beatty in *The Roman Spring of Mrs. Stone*, directed by José Quintero, 1961
(Fondazione Cineteca Italiana)

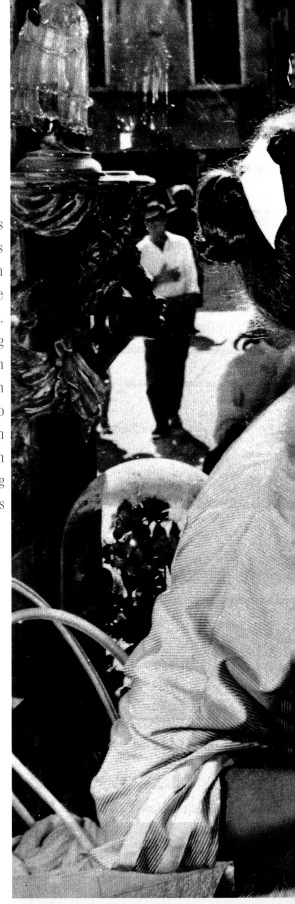

Katharine Hepburn and Rossano Brazzi
in Summertime, directed by David Lean,
1955

(Fondazione Cineteca Italiana)

between early-twentieth-century Sicily and the mob-created Las Vegas of the 1950s was the theme of Francis Ford Coppola's *The Godfather, Part II* (1974). As in *Big Night*, Italy is shown here to be the source of a system of values more personal and more exacting than those of mainstream American culture. Unlike *Big Night*, *The Godfather, Part II* shows these foreign values—some noble, most cruel—succeeding and strongly influencing American culture.

The 1970s were a humbling decade for Americans, a time of oil shortages, military defeat, rampant inflation, and collapsing currency. Although commentators said at the time that the United States had lost its triumphalist attitude and had become more "European," there are no movies that document it. Perhaps that's because Italy had become more expensive for filmmakers, just as it had for tourists. But *Breaking Away* (1979), a film set entirely in Bloomington, Indiana, affirmed that a change had taken place. Dave, its main character, is a cycling prodigy who seems headed nowhere in life and dreams of escape. His fantasy is to be Italian. He irks his parents by bursting into Italian at home. He almost succeeds in seducing a young woman with his stories of missing his mama and papa back in Napoli. This is a major reversal of American mythology. America has always been the place to realize your dreams. Nobody dreamed of escaping to Italy.

But when the Cinzano cycling team comes to Bloomington, the members ignore

Dave. While the United States welcomes people who want to be Americans, Italians know who is Italian, and wannabes from Indiana don't qualify. Even worse, when Dave threatens to win the race, the Italians cheat. Dave's illusions are shattered. (Disillusioning innocents is something Italians often do in English-language fiction and film.) Along with Dave, we have learned that Italians are no better than the rest of us. The American dream is dead, and there's no Italian dream to take its place. But there's one other thing we can't help noticing: those Italian guys wear really great outfits.

Audrey Hepburn and Gregory Peck in
Piazza di Spagna in Roman Holiday,
directed by William Wyler, 1953

(Fondazione Cineteca Italiana)

Dorothy McGuire and Rossano Brazzi in Three Coins

in the Fountain, directed by Jean Negulesco, 1954

I Discovered Italy in America

Alberto Baccari

It was my first trip to America, sometime in the 1970s. I was driving through Montana; I was somewhere in the great American nowhere. I was having a beer at a bar, surrounded by cowboys—a typical saloon. On the television: *Charlie's Angels,* a classic. Suddenly—a commercial. In a very old-fashioned kitchen, dating from the 1950s, even though this was the 1970s, a fat gentleman with a huge Stalin-style mustache sat behind a large, rough-hewn wooden table. He was laughing, with an enormous napkin wrapped around his neck, happily digging into a vast plate of spaghetti overflowing with red sauce and meatballs. "Mamma Mia! That's a spicy meatball," said the "Mustache Pete," his mouth full of spaghetti. After his first bite, however, the director of the commercial steps into the scene, yelling "Cut" and telling the Mustache Pete to put a little more oomph into the scene. He had to be more Italian; he had to move his hands a bit more, laugh louder. Lights . . . camera . . . action! The crew had replaced the plate of spaghetti with a new one, still overflowing with sauce. The Mustache Pete gesticulates wildly,

with both hands, as if invoking divine intervention. He chuckles, and then says, again, "Mamma Mia! That's a spicy meatball," and shovels another enormous forkful of spaghetti into his mouth. Cut. Reshoot. We still don't quite have it. The director criticizes the Mustache Pete actor once again.

They redo the scene at least three more times. Mustache Pete, by this time, is in agony from all the forkfuls of spaghetti with meatballs. He could no longer even repeat his admittedly short lines. This commercial, I learned years later, won many awards. It is one of the most famous pieces of advertising in the world. That was the image of Italy on Madison Avenue. I said to myself, "Advertising is shallow. Advertising people are shallow. Americans are shallow." I thought to myself: this is the complete mass-marketing of an image of Italian immigrants imported to America by boat. It was what the Italians had brought with them, with so much love, carefully protected and preserved; it was all that carried them through so many difficulties and hardships, uncertainties and new challenges in the New World. It was the product of years of exposure of the Americans to customs that came from far-off Sicily, Calabria, Campania, Basilicata, and so on.

For years and years, that specific sort of immigration had contributed to the creation of the image of Italy. In a scene from the Disney movie *Lady and the Tramp,* the male dog, in order to impress the female, takes her to dinner in an alley behind a charming Italian restaurant, where they are

Lavazza 1997 Calendar

Photograph by Albert Watson

(Courtesy Lavazza Spa)

Opposite:

Advertising campaign for Martini France 1996

Photograph by Steve Hiett

(Courtesy McCann-Erickson Paris)

"Rally nell'anima" commercial for Seat Ibiza showing the Tuscan landscape, 1998

(Courtesy Bates Italia Spa—BRW & Partners)

MADE IN ITALY*

MARTINI

*Elaboré en Italie

L'ABUS D'ALCOOL EST DANGEREUX POUR LA SANTÉ, CONSOMMEZ AVEC MODÉRATION

served spaghetti and meatballs. The chef smiles happily at the two dining dogs, and he has the exact same mustachioed face as the Mustache Pete actor in the commercial. In *Pinocchio*, too, Stromboli, the brutal character who kidnaps the marionette, was Italian. He was fat; he gesticulated like a madman; he laughed when there was absolutely nothing to laugh at; and he had a mustache, like the actor and the chef.

And yet I was born in Rome, and I have relatives from Naples. How can it be that I have never even seen a plate of spaghetti and meatballs? In some sense, I always had a hard time taking that excessively ethnic vision of the Italians seriously, all tomatoes and garlic, flasks of wine and red-checkered tablecloths. This ironic vision sprang, and still springs, from the streets of Brooklyn and Little Italy. It was further used by the advertising industry in testimonials to the claimed originality of some pseudo-Italian product that was actually made in New Jersey, and its use began to expand until it was identified as the prototype for a romantic situation. And so the stereotype was used in a commercial for a two-door automobile, featuring an American couple, in a typical Italian restaurant, of course, with a red-and-white-checkered tablecloth, happy, careless, laughing like idiots, to the sound of two singers with a mandolin, pouring out a heartbreaking "O sole mio." There was nothing to be done. That's amore!

For Americans, Italy—from the Alps in the north to the island of Lampedusa in the south—was one unbroken chain of laughing and joking and eating spaghetti with meatballs, with pounds and pounds of garlic and parmesan cheese, with the music of mandolins, all of it seasoned with just a pinch of Mafia —nicely aged Mafia, however. For an Italian, the situation was not a cheerful one.

At the beginning of the 1980s, I too decided to move to the New World—the last in a recent immigration. Many Americans who had arrived before us would say: "You came by air. Not by sea." In the early 1980s, things were looking brighter for the Italians in America. These were the first years of "Made in Italy." In Italy, people were beginning to say, things were being run by the Socialists, who knew how to work internationally. On this side of the Atlantic, people began to talk about Armani, Versace (pronounced Vur-satch-ee, for some reason), and many other designers who were beginning to fill the newspapers with their advertisements. In the space of a few years, fat grandmothers—big wooden spoons glued to their hands, constantly in the kitchen making meatballs—began to be replaced by well-built young models (male and female, but in any case mostly Americans) who began to represent the new image of Italian fashion in the mass media of America. This genetic mingling led to the generation of a new testimonial: a new Italian woman, still in the kitchen, still surrounded by burners and bunches of garlic, sauces all around her, but definitely younger and slimmer. It was the dawning of a new age, a new renaissance.

Fashion was not alone in contributing to the change in the image of Italy. Design did its part as well, of course. From morning to night, there was an endless triumphal procession of modern sofas, hypermodern chairs, and postmodern objets of every kind. Bit by bit, anyone who lived in New York found him- or herself surrounded by new furniture stores selling Italian design. We began to see genuine Italian foodstuffs for sale. There was a massive immigration from regions of Italy that were new to the locals—places like Lombardy, Venetia, and Tuscany. I do not know what time it was or what day it was, but at a certain point the Americans discovered olive oil, especially extra-virgin olive oil. Balsamic vinegar was close behind. Advertising, too, which follows reality at a considerable distance, began to use the image of the New Italy: Northern Italy.

The commercials for products that had anything to do with Italy were suddenly full of Tuscany or Lake Como, with surreal quantities of terra-cotta vases and geraniums always poking up somewhere.

The usual idiotic smiles promoted olive oil, even in spray bottles. The business suits worn by the advertising-agency account executives began to take on amazing, bizarre shapes. The classic executive uniform from Brooks Brothers was being replaced by an Italian suit with four, five, or even six buttons, or even without buttons at all. Businessmen who for years had sweated and squirmed in classic American suits could now feel equally uncomfortable in these awful, oversized pajamas that were "Made in Italy."

The famous "American gigolo" wore clothing designed by Armani. The invasion had even poured over into the small screen of television. Male actors were selling shampoo for greasy hair, all dressed in the same style: very European, very Italian. Sweaters were knotted around their shoulders, their wives and girlfriends wore Todd's shoes, most of their time was spent sitting casually in an open-air café, as if they were in the Piazza Navona, sipping an espresso, naturally smiling like idiots. In short, they were simply "enjoying life" the way Italians do. It was just impossible to take. I wanted to spit. I thought to myself: "Advertising is shallow. Advertising people are shallow. Americans are shallow." I thought to myself: this is the complete mass-marketing of an image of Italian immigrants imported to America . . . by plane. It was what the Italians had brought with them, with so much love, carefully protected and preserved; it was all that carried them through so many difficulties and hardships, uncer-

Alka Seltzer commercial, 1970
DDB Needham agency, U.S.A.

Opposite:
Buitoni advertising campaign, 1996
Photograph by Ferdinando Scianna
(Courtesy McCann-Erickson London)

tainties and new challenges in the New World. It was the product of years of exposure of the Americans to customs that came from far-off Lombardy, Venetia, and Tuscany.

Advertising is shallow. Advertising people are shallow. Americans are shallow. After many years, I went back to Italy. America has everything, but I always felt a lack of something, a yearning. I would wander through the cities like a tourist: Florence, Rome, Naples, Palermo, Milan. And before my astonished eyes, as if by magic, there were Italians everywhere, eating and chatting in the restaurants, in the open-air cafés, with tables crowded with olive oil, extra-virgin olive oil, and even balsamic vinegar.

Everybody was dressed exactly the same way; in fact, everybody wore exactly the same thing. The right jacket, the right dress, the right shirt. Sweaters knotted over their shoulders. Everybody was wearing Todd's shoes.

Scattered around at little tables in open-air cafés, everybody was drinking espresso. They were gesticulating furiously. They were smiling like idiots. Everywhere I looked there were terra-cotta vases and geraniums. I thought to myself:

"When morning filming is terminato, is time for pasta deliziosa and sharing table pleasure."

Buitoni. Share the Italian Love Of Food.

this is the complete mass-marketing of an image born and raised in Italy. It was what the Italians had brought with them, with so much love, carefully protected and preserved; it was all that carried them through so many difficulties and hardships, uncertainties and new challenges in the New World. It was the result of years and years of display, to the Italians, by the Italians, of habits that came from the Italians themselves. I said to myself: Maybe advertising is not all that shallow. And maybe advertising people are not all that shallow. And, just maybe, Americans are not all that shallow, either." But spaghetti with meatballs . . . there is still not a sign of that anywhere.

Visa commercial, U.S.A., 1994,
BBDO NY—D.C. Agency,
Charlie Miesmer & Jimmy Siegel

A Romp in Rome

Fiona Morgan

I was nervous about my stay in Rome. I was to share an apartment for one month in the summer with fourteen other American students in an old palazzo between the Vatican and the Pantheon. The litany of horror stories I'd heard leading up to my departure had created a little film clip of nightmares running through my head: from being relentlessly hounded in the markets to being cornered in an alley, from being groped on a train to being raped in the street. I have problems from time to time in my hometown of Seattle—being followed, propositioned, and yelled at, no matter what I happen to be wearing—so I dreaded what it would be like in Italy. But I figured it was the chance of a lifetime, so I braced myself for the hassles.

Then I talked with a French friend who'd spent two years in Italy. She was baffled by my fear. "Yes, they'll come up and talk to you," Marie said. "They're forward?" I asked. "They are very friendly," she said, "and so attractive!" She shook her hand back and forth, in a French gesture for "woowee."

"You will wish they were interested, but they are only making friends."

By the time I arrived, I didn't know what to expect, and at first I was more concerned with surviving the hustling cab drivers at the Stazione Termini and the frantic traffic as I crossed the street. But before long I came to appreciate the distinctive Roman style Marie had admired: the slick, dark hair and olive skin, the loose, energetic gait of the men in stylish suits or tight jeans, sandals, and sunglasses. As it turned out, these men were forward, but for the most part far from threatening. And their honesty won them points right away.

"You will sleep with me tonight!" said a member of the Italian navy to my friend

Becka after they'd been chatting for a few minutes on the Spanish Steps. "No, no, I have a boyfriend," she replied. "Yes, yes! You will sleep with me tonight!"

The propositions, the whistles, the strange clicking sounds the Roman men made became a fascinating topic of conversation. We looked at their behavior with anthropological curiosity as we read D. H. Lawrence's description of the phallic culture of the Etruscans. These exchanges were part of a larger social flamboyance that is as quintessentially Roman as crumbling stucco, coffee bars, and cobblestones. Rome is like a giant carnival stage, where people speak as much with their gestures as with those words we could barely understand. From our deck and from the crowded streets we watched the old ladies, the richly suited men on fancy Vespas, the punk rockers, the teenage couples making out passionately for all the world to see.

And we realized that bodies take up a different kind of space in Italy—public space. The Italians bump into each other, slide by each other in a crowd, kiss and hug, ride on the backs of each other's mopeds. Bodies are exposed, especially in the July heat that makes even a tank top feel heavy. Bodies surround one another, old and young; they knock into one another, and they mean no harm. Exposed penises and breasts delicately carved in marble line buildings like the Palazzo Spada, a two-minute walk from our apartment. They are whole and revered, a welcome contrast from the disembodied parts splashed on billboards. Even the body of the Virgin Mary, the patron goddess of Rome, is corporeal, represented in infinitely different ways, from ample breasts and round face to the slender hips of a young girl.

"Bella ragazza," a man in white jeans said one day as I walked down a narrow,

Opposite:

Raul Bova

(Grazia Neri)

Illustration by Walter Mollino

for the cover of the family weekly

magazine Grand Hotel, 1950s

shop-lined street. "Ve-ry beau-ti-ful," he said again, looking at my body through my blue cotton dress and then at my face, with a smile. I may not be interested in what he's interested in, I thought, but how could I not smile back at such a compliment?

I felt as though my body were being appreciated rather than attacked. I began to wear the short spaghetti strap dress I had, and the nearly see-through sheer skirt, and not just for the pleasure of the warm wind and sunshine touching my skin—I also anticipated with a little girlish pride the looks and occasional comments I would receive.

What was happening? Was my feminist stamina lapsing? Where was the icy don't-fuck-with-me face, the bitterness of my Seattle pedestrian days? It just wasn't the same. Some of these guys might be lecherous, but they weren't aggressive. For perhaps the first time in my life, I felt safe enough to stop worrying about it. Even when the overall-clad man in the Campo dei Fiori market pinched my ass, my first thought was simply, "Oh yeah, that'll win me over, big boy." His gesture was silly, neither flattering nor threatening. I rolled my eyes and off he went.

Had I treated the place like an amusement park, as some of my young country women did, I might have gotten into trouble. But I found that I could be aware of my surroundings without holding onto my fear.

And by losing that fear, I could be pleasantly surprised by this other system of social behavior. In that month I had more genuine interchanges with Italian men—using the few words I knew of their language or their few words of mine—in bars and shops and out under that bright sun than I have in a year with American men.

Now that I'm back on the streets of Seattle, some of the shields are up again, because the fun is gone. For starters, "Hey, baby" doesn't have quite the same ring as "Ciao, bella." But there's also an anger behind the eyes of the men here, a barely concealed resentment. Catcalls here don't mean the same thing. Those Campo boys would never shout "bitch," either. The old feminist refrain comes back to me: it's not about sex; it's about power.

I'm sick of that refrain; I'd rather understand what's driving the behavior. But seeing one's own culture is always more difficult. For now, I simply content myself with the knowledge that it isn't like this everywhere.

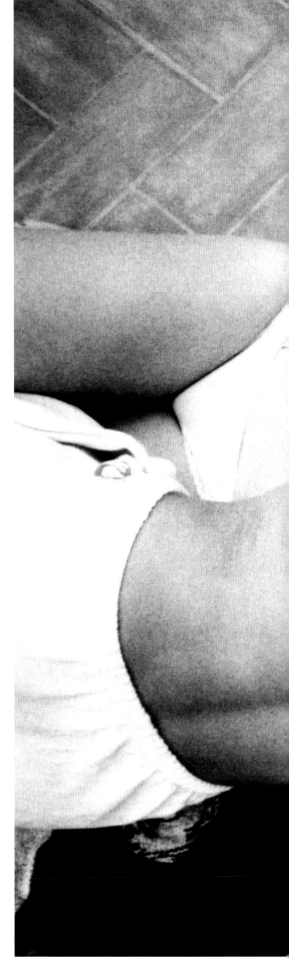

"Vacances à l'italienne," Portofino, 1986

Photograph by Claude Nori

143

Tiramisushi

Kaoru Tashiro

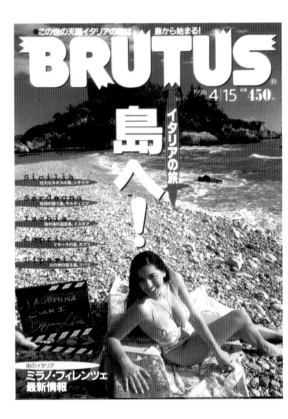

Cover of the Japanese magazine Brutus, April 1996

(Courtesy Brutus, Tokyo)

Opposite:

Italian food in the pages of the Japanese magazine Brutus,
September 1997

The cropping of the photograph underscores the
Japanese interpretation of Italian cuisine.

(Courtesy Brutus, Tokyo)

How to Become an Italian

In 1968 a Los Angeles publisher brought out a book entitled *How to Be an Italian*. It was a manual that attempted to set forth techniques whereby one might appear to be Italian. It was a funny book, full of irony and wit, and it pulled the reader into a whirlpool of wacky humor. And just what characteristics marked the Italians, making them unique?

From northern Italy to southern Italy, and all the way down, across the Strait of Messina, to Sicily, this is the birthplace of a certain distinct form of personal identity, an effort to master the ways of love, a highly visual form of language, and a strong and provocative "body language," a full-fledged commentary on lovemaking, Italian-style. The author of the book an American of Italian descent, appears to be from a Sicilian family. While an Italian would surely furrow his brow at the contents of the book, stereotypical images often contain kernels of truth. This is what the Americans, individuals born into a racial melting pot, think of the Italians; it is, after all,

writers who set out to seek their origins. But those writers are not always successful in that search. The Belgians are the butt of jokes by the French, the Irish are the butt of jokes by the English, but the meaning of this book is not entirely limited to the joke for its own sake; there is a sincere feeling of affection for the Italians throughout the book. All the same, it is necessary to establish a certain distance between the observer and the object under observation.

Italy as an Ideal Superstructure

To Americans, Italy is a homogeneous nation, both in terms of culture and in terms of the natural solidarity with its people. Isn't there something familiar about all this to the Japanese? Older Japanese people remember Italy as an Axis ally from World War II. At times, older Japanese still tell the following anecdote: after the war, if a German and a Japanese happened to meet, one would whisper to the other, "Next time, we'll leave out Italy." And yet this story is not meant to portray the Italians as bumblers; rather it

1
Grissini
●グリッシーニ
名はピエモンテ方言（紐状の）に由来。

2
Michetta
●ミケッタ
中は空洞。ミラノっ子はカリカリが好き。

3
Ferrarese
●フェッラレーゼ
フェッラーラ地方のパン、食感はハード。

4
Pane Pugliese
●プーリアのパン
大きくて平たく白い、セモリナ粉のパン。

5
Pane Toscano
●トスカーナのパン
味の濃い肉料理などに合う無塩パン。

6
Carta da musica
●五線紙パン
極薄で、バリバリという音からこの名が。

Giovanni Galli
●Via Victor Hugo, 2 Milano
☎02・86464833. 8時30分～13時、14時30分～20時30分、日曜休。8月はほぼ夏休み。ミラノに計3店。
左／この店の看板商品は自家製のマロングラッセ。中にホオズキが入ったチョコもイタリアでは人気。

2・8 ロンバルディア
1・11 ピエモンテ
3 エミリア・ロマーニャ
7 リグーリア
4 プーリア
5・9・10 トスカーナ
6 サルデーニア
12 シチリア

Cattaneo Emilio
●Pizza Wagner,13 Milano
☎02・462384. 6時30分～13時30分、16時～19時30分、日曜・月曜午後休。8月は夏休み。
右／オリジナルのそば粉パンが店のお薦め。粉がぎっしり詰まりかなり重い。五穀パン、もろこしパンも。

7
Amaretti teneri di Sassello
●サッセッロ産ソフト・アマレット
8の変形。こっちはスポンジに浸して。

8
Amaretti di Saronno
●サロンノ産アマレット
甘いアンズの酒に浸した固いビスケット。

9
Cantuccini alla mandorla
●アーモンド入りカントゥッチーニ
甘いヴィン・サントに浸しながら食す。

10
Panforte Nannini
●パンフォルテ
シエナ名産。ナッツなどが詰まりリッチ。

11
Gianduia
●ジャンドゥイア
トリノ名産のハシバミの実風味のチョコ。

12
Marzapane
●マジパン
結構グロテスクな色と形が好まれるよう。

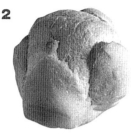

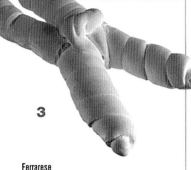

ど こでも買えるといっても、各州ものが揃うのはやはりこだわった店に限られるのだ。

ミラノの高級リストランテ、〈アイモ・エ・ナディア〉のご主人が教えてくれたのが、〈カッターネオ・エミリオ〉。この地で100年以上オープンする店で、各州パンを作ったり取り寄せたりするだけでなく、現代人に合わせたダイエットパンなど常に新しい試みを行っている。

一方、菓子店はドゥオモ近く。〈ペック〉もあるこの地区は、高級な味覚が揃うことで知られる。昔ながらの作りの〈ジョヴァンニ・ガッリ〉は1900年からの老舗。特製のチョコレートが評判だが、イタリア各州の名産も揃えている。空港で慌てて買うならこちらでの物色がお薦め。

conceals a subconscious sense of admiration, a recognition of the Italians' antimilitary nature, their inability to adhere to a senseless and warmongering alliance.

The fundamental, underlying structures of modern Japanese society are based largely on the structures of Anglo-Saxon and German society, while the superstructure is based on Italian society. The Japanese have a deep admiration for the way that Italian society developed and for that society's achievements. Italy is seen in Japan as the homeland of art and architecture, the center from which the Renaissance flourished, a place of sumptuous opera houses and, above all, the cradle of classical culture. The differences between these cultures are so deep that at first one is hard put to find any shared elements. We have no choice, then; we must bow, paying homage to the culture of a distant land: Italy.

The Background of the Boom

Just when was it that the Japanese began to sense a certain familiarity with Italian culture? The first signals appeared in the form of Italian cooking. If we look back in time, we see that Italy was first known in Japan only as the Italy of the Americans. For instance, the first pasta in the Japanese market had trademarks such as "Oh, My Spaghetti" and "Mama Spaghetti." In the 1970s, the Japanese were introduced to the culinary delights of pizza from the chain of Shakey's Pizza, with tabasco sauce and curry flavorings. "Naporitan spaghetti" was served with chopped frankfurters, green peppers, and onions sautéed with ketchup, not tomatoes. Instead of fresh Parmesan cheese, powdered Parmesan was widely used. Japanese cappuccino was topped with whipped cream and a sprinkle of cinnamon. It was the beginning of the 1970s, the golden age of fast food, and Italian cooking began to make itself known in that form—fast food. Enshrined in the respectable niche of slow food, at the same time, was French cuisine, solidly in possession of its preeminent identity as a first-class cuisine. As for other Western cuisines

"à la japonaise," there was a wild and eclectic profusion of curry rice, spaghetti with meat sauce, *kotoletten*, and *omuraisu* (rice omelette).

The preference of the Japanese for French cuisine has venerable roots—modern painting, philosophy, café culture, and, not least, French fashion. Even now, when a Japanese person wishes to give himself or herself romantic airs, or even to be a bit of a snob, he or she will speak of France. Why should this still be the case?

In particular, when Japanese tourists run into each other in Paris, they do their best to avoid each other, with clear expressions of distaste, a distinctive feature of Japanese expatriates. Why is it so common for the Japanese to be ashamed of themselves? This is not a problem limited to the individual in Japan; often the Japanese betray a useless inferiority complex on a collective level. To the extent that they are able, the Japanese attempt to shed their own identity and to become French.

Escape from a National Inferiority Complex

I believe that one path out of this arid inferiority complex with respect to Western nations is offered to the Japanese by Italy. The Italians, conservative though they may be, are relatively free of prejudices against other nations. As one walks down an Italian street, one might feel curious eyes watching one's back—it may well be because you are wearing something strange today, or it might even be mere curiosity. With the growing number of Japanese tourists in Italy, there is a growing volume of information on this subject.

Aside from occasional incidents of price gouging or rude taxi drivers, the impressions that most Japanese visitors describe upon their return from Italy are largely positive. It may happen from time to

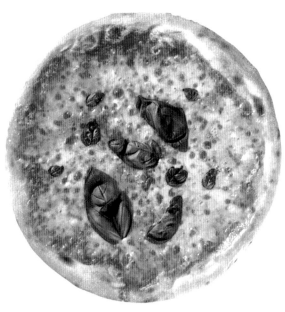

★MARGHERITA
マルゲリータ
1889年6月11日、宮廷に呼ばれた天才職人が、女王マルゲリータに捧げるためにトマトソースの赤、モッツァレッラの白、バジリコの緑でイタリア国旗に見立てたこのピッツァを発明。現在ではナポリ・ピッツァの代名詞。

★ORTOLANA
オルトラーナ
トマトソースと相性のよい野菜ばかりを載せたヘルシーなピッツァ。ナス、ピーマン、ズッキーニは前菜用にあらかじめ網焼きされたものを使用。生ハムを追加できる店もある

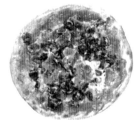

★REGINA
レジーナ
生ハムとマッシュルームをトッピングした、名づけて「ピッツァの女王」。現在でも決して安くはない生ハムだが、ひと昔前は貴重品。庶民には手の届かぬ高嶺の花だったのだ

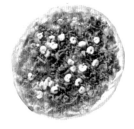

★FRANCESCO
フランチェスコ
小エビとルーコラのサラダといえば、ハイクラスのレストランで出される前菜。それをそのままトッピングしたのがこのピッツァ。洗練されたルックスと味わいの逸品だ

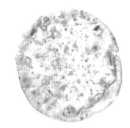

★QUATTRO FORMAGGI
クアットゥロ・フォルマッジ
パルミジャーノ、モッツァレッラ、ゴルゴンゾーラ、それにクリーミーなタレッジョの4つのチーズが溶け合い強烈な風味を醸し出すリコッタやスカモルツァを加える店もある

Pizza "alla sushi" from the Japanese magazine Brutus, September 1996

(Courtesy Brutus, Tokyo)

時代の流れが素材を変える。ピッツァ大図鑑。

●写真／RAFFAELE DONNARUMMA

ピッツァの発祥地はナポリ。最初はマリナーラやマルゲリータのようなシンプルなものしかなかったけれど、時代を追うごとにトッピングのバリエーションもこんなにたくさん出てきた。ここに紹介しているピッツァはミラノの〈ダ・プルチネッラ〉で撮影したもの。イタリアでは定番ピッツァ以外は、ほとんどが各店のオリジナルピッツァを提供しているので、このページではバリエーションが豊富なこのお店のいろんなピッツァを目で味わっていただきたい。

...TTI DI MARE
...ッティ・ディ・マーレ

...小エビ、ムール貝をふんだんに...の香りがするピッツァ。イタリ...されるカニかまもプラス。モ...を使うかどうかは賛否両論。

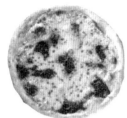

★GENOVESE
ジェノヴェーゼ

パスタによく使われるジェノヴァ風ペーストを使用。バジリコ、松の実、ニンニク、山羊のチーズ、オリーブオイル、クルミで作るクラシックな味はピッツァ生地にもよく合う。

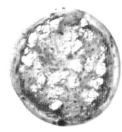

★ROMANA
ロマーナ

トマトソース、モッツァレラ、原乳からチーズを採った残りかすで作るリコッタチーズを載せる。昔は羊乳のリコッタを使ったが、今はあっさりした牛乳で作るのが一般的。

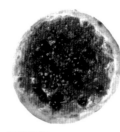

★SICILIANA
シチリアーナ

トマトソース、ケッパー、オリーブ、アンチョビ、オレガノのトッピングはすべてシチリアの名産。オリーブは若い緑の実ではなく、成熟した黒い芳醇なものを使うのが決まりだ。

...RK

...ツの首相ビスマルクは目玉焼き...キが大好きだった。それをピ...したのがこれ。肉の代わりに生...わりに配している。

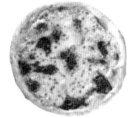

★TIROLESE
ティロレーゼ

山羊の乳から作るチロル地方名産のカプリーノチーズ、生ハムの一種・スペック、苦みが強く繊細やかなルーコラ、そしてモッツァレッラを存分にちりばめた贅沢なピッツァ。

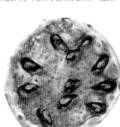

★TARANTINA
タランティーナ

タラントはムール貝の養殖で有名な南イタリアの町。魚介類のピッツァではモッツァレッラを抜く場合が多いが、写真のように使用すれば貝殻にトマトソースが焦げつかない。

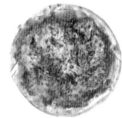

★NAPOLI
ナポリ

アンチョビで塩味とうまみを加え、オレガノで生臭さを消しつつ香りを強化したピッツァ。マルゲリータ誕生直後、ナポリ人の創造力が生み出したバリエーションのひとつ。

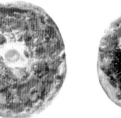

...RO STAGIONI
...コ・スタジオーニ

...節に見立てたピッツァ。写真...ッシュルーム、オリーブ、アー...使っているが、店によっては...取って替わることも。

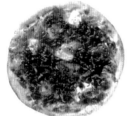

★PUGLIESE
プリエーゼ

ほどよく焼けたタマネギの甘みに、焦げかけたパルミジャーノの風味がベストマッチ。ほかにはトマトソースしか使わないシンプルな一品。名称はタマネギの産地プーリアから。

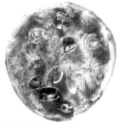

★POSILLIPO
ポジリッポ

生アサリが窯の中で口を開き、うまみたっぷりのジュースがチーズの上に広がる。水っぽくなく焼き上げるのが難しい。ポジリッポはアサリの養殖が盛んだったナポリの海岸地方。

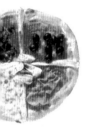

...RESE

...の州カラブリア名産の、とっ...ラシ入りサラミをトッピング...ので「悪魔のピッツァ」とも...パテで食欲がない時にイチ押し。

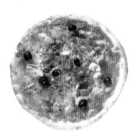

★CAPRICCIOSA
カプリッチョーザ

生ハム、オリーブ、アーティチョーク、ケッパー、アンチョビに、普通はマッシュルームとゆで卵も加える。名前はわがままな人も満足させる、という意味がこめられている。

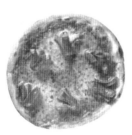

★TEDESCA
テデスカ

ウィンナーソーセージをたっぷり載せた新世代のピッツァ。若者に人気で、今やどこのピッツァ屋でも見られる。食に閉鎖的なイタリアにおいても食文化は変わりつつある？

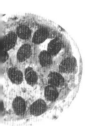

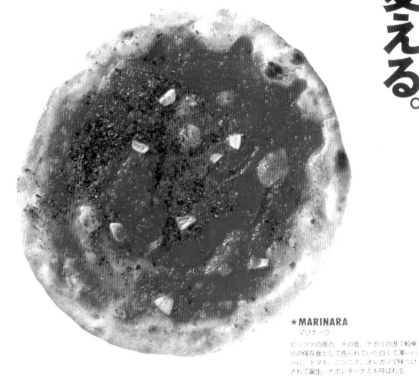

★MARINARA
マリナーラ

ピッツァの原点。その昔、ナポリの港で船乗りの保存食として売られていた白くて薄いパンに、トマト、ニンニク、オレガノで味つけされて誕生。ナポレターナとも呼ばれる。

---

time that something is stolen from a Japanese tourist; if it is done with style and cunning. there may even be a sneaking sense of admiration on the part of the victim. And yet, upon his or her return to Japan, the victim of the theft will describe the episode to his or her friends in outsized detail, por-traying it as an exceptional experience. In Italy, one has the feeling that everything is bound up with the world of the senses. And so, in the 1980s, the Japanese—in an almost wholly natural manner—finally found a foreign culture that fit in perfectly with their way of life: Italian fashion and Italian cuisine.

Lingua di manzo in salsa verde
●牛タンの緑野菜ソースがけ
パセリ、タマネギ、ツナなどのソース。

Insalata di formaggi
●チーズのサラダ
モッツァレラを使用。クルミは気分で。

Gnocchi alla romana
●ローマ風ニョッキ
普通はイモだが、ローマ風はセモリナ粉。

Lasagne al forno
●ラザーニャ
これと上の2品だけが毎日登場する定番。

Ravioli salsa aurora
●ラビオリのオーロラソース
生クリーム、トマト、チーズのソース。

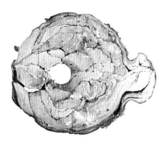

Porchetta
●ローストポーク
直径20cmはある輪切り状態の豚。

The universality of these two products, the ease with which they could be assimilated, rapidly became clear to the Japanese. And everything coincided with the phase of the most spectacular expansion of Japan's *baburu* (bubble economy).

The Birth of the Katarogu Bunka (The Culture of the Catalog)

In the second half of the 1980s, in the world of Japanese magazines Italy boldly took center stage. Beginning with fashion, moving on to cooking and wines, and all the way down to industrial design, the attention of the Japanese public has focused on products from each area of cultural endeavor. Because the Japanese are exceedingly sensitive to which things are "in" and which are "out," consumer goods can become "in" with astonishing rapidity. It is enough for an "in" product to be placed on sale, and in the blink of an eye, the shelves are swept clean.

Because of the structure of Japanese consumer culture (which is extremely brand-conscious), when a product becomes a cult object among the mass consuming public, that product quickly sells in astounding numbers. This is an important factor that bears keeping in mind, because a product can shift from the status of "in" to that of "out" at blinding speed, and so it is important to keep an eye on consumer behavior. This social mechanism, in many cases, is triggered by magazines.

Magazines (at times, in the form of catalogs), not television, are the prime channel for the transmission of information on the characteristics of products and for the involvement of consumers. More than any other source of information, it is magazines that provide recommendations and play a crucial role in indicating which products are "in." Open any magazine to any page and you will find a layout

made up of just information and cropped photographs.

Young Japanese people who travel to Italy bring with them clippings from magazines and photographs of suits, consumer goods, and even food. Pointing at the photograph, they repeat: "Questo, per favore." When "questo" is not available, however, a problem arises. A product that has not been published, even if it bears the same trademark, is unknown to these young consumers, and they cannot tell whether it is "good" or not.

A real problem, on the other hand, is determining what will become fashionable. "Tsuhan seikatsu" (a mail-order catalog) sold both De Longhi ovens and pillows certified to come from Italian hospitals, and both were genuine bestsellers. At times, it happens that a dessert may become popular. In 1990, the magazine *Hanako* published an article on tiramisu, triggering a full-fledged tiramisu feeding frenzy. All the pastry shops in Japan began to make tiramisu, and by the peak of the frenzy it was possible to buy tiramisu-flavored chewing gum; just a year later, the tiramisu fever had begun to subside. Immediately, however, the public's attention focused on panna cotta, and all of the Japanese seemed to be involved in a competition to find the best panna cotta.

When a product becomes so popular, anyone who is not familiar with this product is quickly branded an "outsider." In Japan both Prada and panna cotta are equally famous. The difference is that Prada is always very "in," while the euphoria over that particular dessert is already "out."

The Culture of the Otaku

There are scholars of Italian culture, impassioned to the point of fanaticism, who are known in Japan as *otaku*. After a first phase, in which Italian cuisine appeared in various distorted manifestations, young people made every effort to catch up, and set out in search of genuine Italian cooking. At the end of the 1980s, the most refined Italian fine food shops, such as Il Salumaio di Montenapoleone or Peck, made their way to Tokyo. Raw materials that had been unknown in Japan until just a short time ago are now produced and sold, even in the supermarkets.

There was a time when the Italians who came to Japan brought a suitcase full of *pastasciutta* with them; now this precaution is needless. Barilla and De Cecco—of course—but even handmade pasta from Italy has become a cult product, and Latini pasta can be found even in department stores. Young chefs who serve apprenticeships in the finest Italian restaurants come back to Japan, where they open their own restaurants. That there are more than five thousand Italian restaurants throughout Japan (Italian chefs are a tiny minority) should be something that surprises even the Italians themselves. Italian cuisine has given French cuisine a sharp bounce from the pedestal, where it once stood as the unquestioned champion, and now France trails behind piteously.

The Bursting of the "Bubble"

Magazines continue to publish numerous articles on Italian cooking and wine, despite the onslaught of the economic crisis. And these are not specialty magazines. *Brutus*, a Japanese biweekly aimed at a male readership, devotes each issue to a specific subject that is analyzed in every detail.

Seventy percent of each issue of the 130-page magazine is devoted to the main theme. This magazine has contributed greatly to a spread of knowledge and understanding of Italian cooking and wine. The food articles are not limited to an exploration of the dishes and recipes of regional Italian cuisine; they go on to focus on various personalities from the world of restaurants. For example, in 1996, it was the members of the Associazione Pizza Autentica of Naples; in 1997, the great food expert Vincenzo Buonassisi; and then, in 1998, the president of the Gambero Rosso guides, Stefano Bonilli, and his wife (they were in Japan to work on classifying Japan's Italian restaurants and pizzerias). The magazine serves as a full-fledged manual and, because of the crisis, is read very closely.

The Italians of an Italy That Does Not Exist

Should we assume that young Japanese want to become like Italians? Certainly not. How could they live with the awareness that, however much they may envy the Italians, life in Italy is inconvenient? They could never live in a place with no stores open twenty-four hours a day, where it is impossible to go shopping on Sunday, where there are no automatic vending machines every thirty feet. It is not so much a matter of becoming Italian; rather it is a question of adapting a certain Italian style to the everyday Japanese way of life. For the Japanese, it is a perfectly natural thing to be: a little bit Italian, a little bit French, a little Indian, Chinese, Korean, and, last of all, a little bit Japanese, immersed in a sort of ethnic and cultural schizophrenia.

It may be pointed out that the Japanese understanding of Italy is still quite superficial. But can we not compare the character of a country to the character of a Tower of Babel, jammed with astonishing individuals? Clothing, cooking, furniture and interior decoration, art, literature—which of these should be considered the most important field?

The most important thing, in any case, is not a trademark or a consumer product, but what underlies the production of either, the passion and dedication with which the craftsman has labored. So we can sit down to a meal and savor the moment of joy of being one with the Italians. This is the surest path to an understanding and an experience of Italy. The opportunities are at hand, and is this not—in the final analysis—what the magazines are whispering?

Cotoletta alla milanese
●ミラノ風カツレツ
さすがに本場、薄くてデカイ。仔牛のカツ。

Mozzarella in carrozza
●モッツァレラのはさみ揚げ
中にバジルなどが入っている。

Pomodori alla piastra
●トマトのグリル
グリル自慢の店だけあり、ひと味深い。

Trevisana alla piastra
●トレヴィザーナのグリル
イタリア独特の葉野菜を焼いたもの。

Macedonia di verdure
●野菜のマチェドニア
季節の野菜たくさんのオイルマリネ。

Pesche all'amaretto
●アマレット風味のピーチ
アマレットはアンズの核から作る食後酒。

Cucina Italiana & New American Cuisine

David Le Boutillier

For the first half of the twentieth century, most Americans thought of Italian cuisine in terms of the rough peasant cooking brought to the United States. by ragged immigrants fleeing the poverty of southern Italy. In fact, in the twenty years between 1890 and 1910, about five million southern Italians poured into the United States. According to the food writer John Mariani, "The key to understanding Italian food culture in the United States is knowing where the Italians immigrants came from—80 percent were from south of Rome."

Those southern Italian immigrants brought with them a simple cuisine—a cuisine far more Mediterranean than European—based largely on vegetables, fruit, beans, and grains. They had been poor, even by Italian standards, and their daily meals reflected that fact. However unpretentious the ingredients, the food was hearty, fresh, and easy to like. As the playwright Neil Simon once observed, "There are two laws in the Universe: the Law of Gravity, and Everybody Likes Italian Food." That statement is both accurate and misleading: Italian food is indeed generally well liked. But, in a very real sense, there is no such thing as "Italian food."

First off, Italy has as many cuisines as it has provinces, regions, cities, and dialects (that is, quite a few). Second, even that intensely intricate body of culinary culture has been refracted and multiplied in its incarnation in the United States. Many of the early culinary arrivals—southern Italian recipes—were modulated for the broader American palate of the period (we should keep in mind that the American palate changed over time, just as Italian cuisine did). Meat became more prominent, to satisfy a nation of meat eaters. Traditional spaghetti dishes were served with meatballs—unheard of in Italy, where meat and pasta were separate courses. Veal cutlets and veal chops became common staples. Other traditional dishes such as eggplant parme-

TAGLIARINI TAGLIATELLI
VERMICELLI CRESCIONI DITALINI RAVIOLI PENNE MACARONI
REGINETTE STRICHETTI TAGLIARI
TAGLIATELLI TORTELLINI LINGUINE CANERINI
TAGLIARINI STRICHETTI REGINETTE
VERMICELLI CRESCIONI DITALINI RAVIOLI REGINETTE STRICHETTI TAGLIARINI TAGLIATELLI

san or zucchini parmesan morphed into chicken parmesan.

Some dishes that we consider classic items on any Italian menu, such as Caesar salad, pasta primavera, and shrimp scampi, were all developed with the American diner in mind. Caesar salad was actually the brainchild of Caesar Cardini, a restaurateur who concocted the dish in 1924 on the Fourth of July at his restaurant in Tijuana, Mexico, for visiting movie stars. The Hollywood folk then popularized Caesar salad back home, and in time it became popular around the country.

Other dishes were named after Italian villages "back home" or world-famous Italian personalities. Chicken Tetrazzini, for instance, a dish of chicken and cream sauce over spaghetti, was named after Italian soprano Luisa Tetrazzini.

By midcentury, following World War II, a new window opened onto Italian culture; art films provided a different image of Italian society. After decades of knowing only the lower classes that had fled Italy, Americans were introduced to the Italian upper-class lifestyle through such avant-garde films as Federico Fellini's *La Dolce Vita* and Jean-Luc Godard's *Contempt.* (At the time, Italy had virtually no middle class, only upper and lower; but that was to change rapidly over the next decade, still remembered in Italy as the post-war boom or the economic miracle.)

Borrelli's Italian restaurant

Long Island, New York

"Come and Taste the Best of Italy"

Rigoletto

In addition to these new views of Italian society, the Italian art films introduced the American public to an aspect of Italian culture that would ultimately change restaurant culture in America for good: the lobby café. The lobby of the art-film theater became a cultural forum, a place to talk politics and art and culture—all distinctly non-American things to do. European café society was introduced to New York. The central theme of the lobby was, of course, the espresso bar, with its spectacular espresso machine, suddenly an icon of all that was European and modernist.

Whatever gewgaws may have been shown off in the theater lobbies in the 1950s, most Italian restaurants in America were small family operations; many began life as a grocery store or bar with a couple of tables, eventually developing into a full-service restaurant. Patronage might be limited to family and friends; it only gradually expanded beyond the boundary of the neighborhood.

Most early immigrants had no prior restaurant experience and simply fell into the business. As a result, their restaurants were sparse and simple, with family memorabilia and photographs as the sole decorations. Over time, as Italian restaurants grew in popularity, interiors began to reflect a vernacular culture rather than any specific images relating to the family's actual ancestral heritage. Sentimental murals depicted the

Italian food products in a plate glass window in Manhattan

Photograph by Leslie Fratkin

Bay of Naples or gondolas slipping down a Venetian canal, providing warm romantic imagery that appealed to American sensibilities. In time, Americans would come to feel ill at ease in any Italian restaurant that lacked the requisite red-and-white-checkered tablecloths and straw-covered Chianti bottles with candles dripping wax. Perhaps it was a sense of place that Italian-American restaurants provided in a society that famously lacked roots and permanence; perhaps it was the broad-stroke, in-your-face display of effusive romanticism that reinforced the overwhelming appeal of Italian-American cuisine.

Whether it was the theatrical aspects or the deep distrust that Italian-Americans harbored for canned or preserved ingredients—preferring whatever was fresh and in season—Italian restaurants became immensely popular across America. The 1959 opening of New York's Four Seasons (a name reminiscent of both Vivaldi and a certain variety of pizza) by Joe Baum and Restaurant Associates marked a new era in American dining.

Clearly, this was a tremendous departure from the ethnically wrapped family trattorias, and it was scarcely thought of as Italian in any way. Still, the Four Seasons was heavily influenced by Italian imagery, heritage, and food culture. Conceptually, the restaurant was breaking new ground by heralding fine American cuisine; it relied upon the Italian passion for fresh seasonal ingredients for its menu and its namesake.

As summer turned to fall and winter gave way to spring, the chefs at the Four Seasons drew inspiration for new creations from seasonal produce, fish, game, and other ingredients that became available—a clear slap in the face to the culture of frozen foods that attempted to abolish seasonal variations. Even the restaurant's potted plants and the servers' uniforms changed with the seasons.

The Four Seasons also introduced a new aesthetic dimension that would forever change restaurant design and culture. If, as architect

Barocco Italian restaurant ,

New York

Peter Bentel states, "The process of restaurant design is turning nature into culture," that ideal can be seen in the design of the Four Seasons. The project was given to Mies van der Rohe, who turned it over to his associate, Philip Johnson. Despite the modernist credo, "Form follows function," there was an unmistakably Italian sensuousness in the design. Though clearly conceived as American and strongly influenced by modernism, the Four Seasons nonetheless shows a richness and elegance previously absent from American restaurants. The use of sensuous materials evokes a universal response, endowing the space with a very elemental quality. The use of travertine on the floors (earth), shimmering curtains that rippled with the slightest movement (air), the gently gurgling pool in the Pool Room (water), and the majesty of the high ceilings (sky) all recall centuries of Italian craftsmanship and tradition. Although such rich, elegant, and natural materials had been used for centuries in venues such as the Caffè Florian (Venice, 1720), it was clearly an Italian inspiration that brought them to the United States.

Even though the Four Seasons truly pioneered the idea of a seasonally inspired menu (and restaurant concept), much credit has gone (in some cases, rightfully) to a later culinary movement known as the new American cuisine. The most prominent figure in that movement is Alice Waters, who has been described as the mother of new American cuisine. Waters's Berkeley, California, restaurant, Chez Panisse, proffered a new kind of Mediterranean-inspired cooking that was more about the individual ingredients than their sum. Waters's obsession with quality and provenance of food reverberated throughout the menu of Chez Panisse, which was developed and changed daily, depending on the morning's purchases from local purveyors. Waters is said to have returned more food than she accepted at first, until her exacting standards set a new benchmark for purveyors and restaurateurs. It was the persona of chef as artist, as visionary, as devotee of a fresh-foods cult (not unlike the mercurial Primo of the film *Big Night*).

Today, many restaurants wear this philosophy on their sleeves through the use, and often overuse, of descriptive buzzwords on the menu, such as day-boat scallops, organic field greens, heirloom tomatoes, and free-range chicken. Of course, in Italy, and most of the rest of Europe, it is assumed that menu ingredients are fresh and regional. In Italy, in particular, this is more often not a philosophical decision, but one of necessity. Typically, it is the regionalism and the personality of a restaurant that differentiates it from others, not the latest design or concept.

Waters's philosophy was influential, and with other pioneers such as Jeremiah Tower and Wolfgang Puck, American food culture came under the sway of what is now thought of as the new American cuisine or, significantly, the new California cuisine. In *Inventing the Dream*, Kevin Starr pointed out that California was touted from its very inception, at the turn of the century, as America's equivalent of—variously—Athens, the Riviera, the Mediterranean, and Italy. It hardly seems surprising, then, that the new California

uisine should be largely a retooling of the old new American Italian cuisine. Drawing heavily n Italian influences, there was a proliferation of ienu items, ingredients, and even cooking methods not previously seen in this country. Modern iterpretations of pasta dishes, risotto, and, of ourse, pizza sprang up on menus everywhere.

More than a novelty, this "new" cuisine hanged the way Americans eat and think about ood. Hybrid restaurant concepts, such as alifornia Pizza Kitchen, have been formed around he simple idea of using exotic and sometimes utlandish ingredients on a traditional pizza crust, r tossed with a bowl of noodles.

Go to any national grocery-store chain and ou will find twenty varieties of olive oil, sun-dried omatoes, pine nuts, pesto, and even fresh pasta, ll of which were unavailable until recently except, perhaps, from a gourmet food store). olfgang Puck has even released a line of frozen ourmet pizzas for distribution through a national rocery-store chain. Cooking methods, such as

wood-burning ovens and rotisseries, have also been adopted; used for centuries in Italy, they are now revolutionizing American restaurant kitchens. Having said this, Italians would be hard pressed to find anything recognizable on a menu from either Puck's Spago or Waters's Chez Panisse. Despite adopting ingredients and methods, the cuisine remains uniquely American. With the advent of this new cuisine, the way Americans think about restaurants has changed as well. Restaurants have become theater, and the food has become fashion. Restaurants have actually become the destination for an evening's entertainment, not unlike the opera or a symphony. Eating a pizza with grilled chicken, pesto, and sun-dried tomatoes while rubbing elbows with Wolfgang Puck is tantamount to attending a movie premiere with Michael Douglas. No longer is it acceptable to be the temperamental chef behind the scenes, whose only mantra is *la mia cucina*. Restaurants are now a selective mass medium, and the chefs are the stars—or perhaps we should say the divas.

Windows of the Dean & Deluca store, Broadway, New York.

Photograph by Tulla Booth

High Culture, Low Inflation: Italy through Soccer

Alix Sharkey

Italy is regarded by sports journalists the world over as one of the four great soccer-playing nations, along with Brazil, Argentina, and Germany. Having won the World Cup three times and qualified for all but two of the final tournaments since the competition started in 1930, Italy can claim to be one of the stalwarts of the modern international game. However, Italian soccer, or football, has changed greatly over recent years, and with it the image of Italy itself. In particular, Italy's hosting of the World Cup in 1990 was a deliberate exercise in international communications, a way of representing Italy as a bold, adventurous, young nation at the heart of a modern capitalist Europe.

A generation ago Italian football could not possibly have represented such values. For a long time it was regarded as insular, unimaginative, and neurotically rigid in terms of its tactics. *Catenaccio*—"the lock" or "the bolt"— was the style with which Italian football was most strongly associated before Italia '90. Developed by the Inter Milan team of the 1960s, it was a dour and sterile tactic. The idea was to mark the opposition's forwards out of the match, play defensively, and try to snatch a goal on the counterattack once the opposition was over-committed. The *catenaccio* side would then immediately revert to solid defense. The popularity of this tactic meant that the Italian championship regularly recorded the lowest number of goals of any in Europe, with most games ending 0–0 or 1–0. However, the Italian public loved to watch—attendance continued to rise as the game became increasingly popular throughout the 1970s and 1980s.

For the British, *catenaccio* eventually evolved into a complete theory—albeit a self-contradictory one—about the Italian game, and hence the Italian national character. As Peter Davies explains in *All Played Out: The Full Story of Italia '90*, "In football, the British stereotype is that Italians are more clever, more skillful, more technical. Their defenses are more cynically brutal, and superglue-solid; their strikers are rapier-sharp and lazy, drama queens who score on the break and, otherwise, strut about preening and posturing while the hard men do the work at the back. Their play is slow (hot country, idle people) possession football, intelligent, intricate, and tedious. And their manner is melodramatic, hysterical—they're babies, they roll on the turf in fake agony and anguish, they gesture and protest... not British at all. They sit back, poach a goal, then lock the game up at 1–0. And the crowds are nutters, demented, 58 million national team managers. Bring on, at this point, the jokes about how many reverse gears they put in their tanks." (This is a reference to a wartime joke about Italian tanks having six gears, one forward and five reverse: that is, Italians are cowards, too.) Writing in 1990, Davies felt that any kind of balanced view was a rarity.

Supporters of Italy were just as likely as its detractors to lapse into cliché: "People who think they know Italy think either that it's rotten in every regard (P2 and the Mafia, wormy coalitions and psychopathic driving, Fiat and the Pope, scything fouls and injured innocence) or they think it's just too heavenly perfect in every conceivable way. These latter read John Mortimer in Tuscany, drink wine with holiday abandon, rave about the food and the art... the Palio at Siena, the shoes and the clothes and the furniture and the ice-cream, the duomos and saints... and (say) their football's so good, so much style and flair compared to the thunderbolt rubbish we Brits churn out..."

Although the British Premier League is now the world's richest (thanks to revenue generated by selling exclusive television rights to Rupert Murdoch's BSkyB satellite network), Italy remains the mother of modern football as

transcultural spectacle, of football as an international communications event. It is to Italy and Italia '90 that we owe our conception of the World Cup as the great spectacle of our age—one that, we are told, can unite the world's nations, bringing together two-thirds of the human race in a monumental orgy of passion and pride, hope and fear. Certainly Italia '90 rescued football from its darkest moment, restoring its reputation after the ugly events of the 1980s and the tragedies of Heysel, Bradford, and Hillsborough. According to the French cultural theorist Pierre Lanfranchi, "There was a need to halt the sport's decline in popularity and consolidate its traditional image as the sport of the masses which enjoys the largest, most extensive worldwide audience."

The key to Italia '90's success was the Comitato Organizzatore Locale—or Local Organizing Committee—directed by Luca Cordero di Montezemolo, a scion of the Fiat-owning Agnelli family and manager of the Ferrari Formula 1 racing team. Under his direction, the COL skillfully packaged and marketed Italia '90 so that it was perceived, in Britain at least, as a spontaneous and popular expression of national character; there was the impression that the tournament was being funded by the Italian government as a celebration of national character. In fact, Montezemolo initiated a new level of professionalism in manipulating the image of football as a wealth-generating communications tool. From the outset, he believed that the month-long Italia '90 tournament would generate 320 billion lire—then equivalent to $245 million—half of it from ticket sales, the rest coming from sponsors such as

Canon, Coca-Cola, Anheuser-Busch beer, Philips, Fuji Film, Gillette, and JVC. These firms invested 13 billion lire in the organization, with the rest donated, often in terms of goods and services, by official suppliers (all Italian) including Olivetti, the state railway FFSS, the state television company RAI, Fiat, and the National Bank of Labor.

Right from the opening ceremony, Italia '90 set new standards for creativity in terms of communications. But perhaps the COL's most astute move was to refurbish and rebuild the nation's football stadiums, transforming them into worthy temples for the titans of the modern game. Italian stadiums are bigger and better attended than anywhere else in Europe; Milan's San Siro stadium, for example, was already legendary for its size and breathtaking grandeur when Peter Davies visited it in early 1990; even though renovations for Italia '90 were still unfinished, he came away raving: "It's an unbelievable stadium... the San Siro was the greatest stadium I'd ever seen in my life... it's not pretty... a gray brute bulk of a place, and the great mass of the squat spiral pillars outside makes it look like some terrifying kind of alien machine-beast, coiled to spring. It's by Spielberg out of Orwell. It seats 80,000 and it's the closest encounter you'll get to the future of football... I walked on the new grass at the San Siro, under the tall sweep of the empty seats, and I thought—the World Cup starts here? No

problem." Similarly, Pierre Lanfranchi noted: "The stadiums built or rebuilt for Italia '90 were unlike anything the football-going public had seen before... vast, magnificent, functional, elegant... [equipped with] ultra-modern facilities (video screens, telephones, VIP sky boxes)... they represented the 'jewels' of modern architecture, reflecting the Italian genius for design and elegant functionality." Of course, the construction was not without problems, which themselves were regarded by the British as typically Italian in their nature: strikes, interminable delays, accusations of bribery and corruption, and the deaths of several workers when sections of the roof collapsed in Palermo's Stadio della Favorita.

Massive sports stadiums have always reflected a country's economic, social, and political climate. When Italy first hosted the World Cup in 1934, it produced strikingly modern stadiums that symbolized the modernist aspirations of futurism. In a similar way the 1990 constructions were supposed to reflect the increased quality of Italian infrastructure, to eradicate the image of Italy as the backward nation of Europe, to make Italy look dynamic and modern, yet still as passionate and creative as ever, while signifying the individualism of Italian architecture and society.

Consequently, international football became a tool of national expression and international communications, a medium for redefining cultural parameters. Italy sold the rest of the world—and bought back from itself—the image of a vital young nation, capable of competing with the best in the new game of international neoliberal capitalism—where

パローネ[ボール]
pallone

カルチョ この訳語のないイタリア語は
じつはよく頭を知らず・カルチョのカルチョ。サッカー
のこと、複なこともある。トドはに、したサッカーかのト
カルチョはサッカーにのことたくさん・リーグ・ブーム
でもつ未来、という方もあるうろ人、市民感覚にはまだまだ
い。本特集でサッカーとかイタリア・サッカーかという
うり気分ではないとというに紹介するため、初めてで
いうかは是非御記憶の感じ。

セリエA イタリアが世界に誇るサッカ
ー、前のリーグのこと、18チームが前期から後期へ
それぞれのホームグラウンドで、試合ずつ、計36試合が
行われ、勝ち負けと引き分けて、順点と失点の差など
でランキングされる。優勝すると、翌年度チャンピオン
ズ・カップという、ヨーロッパ№1チームを決める大
会に出場し、さらにこのチ優勝すると、翌年12月の
東京で行われるトヨタカップにやってくる。

メルカート といえば普通は「市場」の
ことだが、ここではサッカー選手たちの移籍によ
わる会、ウワサ、かけひきのことである。ちなみに
イタリア経済の好き込みに関わらず、選手の年俸な
の高さは世界一、あのマラドーナがナポリというチ
ームに移籍したときが約25億円、ところが今年、レ
ッティー移籍市、ドリの選手が買収選手がAC
ランク何で33億円で誘わられると、社会問題にもなる。

デルビー 英語の「ダービー」のイタリア
式発音、イタリアの都市のほとんどにわが町のチー
ムがあって、完璧な対抗スタイルになっている
が、大都市には2チームがやるところもある。
一リーにはローマとラツィオ、ミラノにはACミランと
チェル、ドリにはユベントスとドリ、ジェノヴァには
ブリアとシェヴァ、シーズンに2回、判はまっこ
つ、これほど盛り上がるものはない。

サッカー が生まれたのは、ストイックな遊び好きなイングランド
ー これをカルチョと呼びこのイタリアでも、アレナトーレ
を「ミスター」といまだに呼んだりする、ラテン民族からの教養とでも言うものでしょ
う、ボール1傷えあればだれてあるなど、きわめて高度で洗練されたゲームを翻ぎ
たのは彼らなのだから、そもそもサッカーの起源としては、隣町町で足を奪いあうというものでも
かわりに蹴りあったとかの有名なエピソードはある。南米では、子供たちがデレ
か布を球状に結いたものので足を蹴いている、という美談(?)もある。しかし、こ
は、革製でしなやかな弾力を持った完璧な球体ボール一バローネが主人公
こいつがなければ何も始まらない。45分ずつ前後半で行われる試合は、このボール
が約11センチメートルの外周分。「一回転」したとき
始まる。スーパースター、アマ
チュア選手たち、子供たち。誰でもボールが、まばゆい軌跡を描く(瞬間、ゴー)

competition was tough but supposedly fair.

As for the quality of the game itself, Italy went into Italia '90 having already established its domestic championship as the epicenter of football excellence. In the preceding two seasons, Italian teams had won five of the six major European competitions; Italy seemed likely to dominate the game for years to come. By 1990, the best players in the world were playing for Italian clubs; a couple of years earlier, Diego Maradona had led lowly Napoli to two *scudetti*, while AC Milan was just entering an era of total domination of European football, during four years when they were powered to a string of titles by the Dutch trio of Gullit, Rijkaard, and Van Basten. This international influence had revolutionized the Italian game: Milan's 4–4–2 team formation, based on the typical British pattern, was the complete inversion of the *catenaccio* system; it emphasized pushing upfield and attacking the opposition,

rather than waiting for them to make a mistake. AC Milan's success convinced other teams to experiment with this radical method, and Arrigo Sacchi, the manager who had introduced it, was appointed national coach for Italia '90.

As far as British fans were concerned, Italy also led the field when it came to producing sportswear. The summer of 1990 saw British dance floors dotted with young men wearing replicas of the shirts of Italian domestic teams, such as AC Milan, Juventus, Internazionale, and Napoli. Another popular choice was the violet Fiorentina shirt, which became a favorite with West London lads. This was partly due to a desire to associate themselves with the game while not wearing partisan domestic colors, and partly because Italian shirts were simply more elegant than anything produced by British clubs at the time.

Italian sports-influenced leisure wear such as Tacchini and Fila had long been popular

Illustration for an article on Italian soccer

From Esquire—Japan, June 1993

Opposite:

"Anything to do with fashion has to be Italy, they say. And football, obviously..."

From the Guardian Weekend, April 4, 1998

Photograph by Martin Parr

(Contrasto)

with football-loving British "casuals" (just as Italian knitwear and motorscooters were favorites with an earlier incarnation of British youth culture, the mods), and a relatively new brand called Kappa was soon being worn by the opinion formers. But it was the Italian team's football shirt that proved most popular. One of the all-time classic football strips, this simple short-sleeved blue shirt with minimal details (a very discreet red, white, and green trim on the collar and cuffs) was the definitive sportswear garment that summer and is still occasionally seen even today on the streets and in the clubs of London.

The COL was the model of a modern enterprise, its liberal, free-market philosophy in line with the tastes of the day. The financial success of Italia '90 was such that immediately after the tournament the organizing committee for the 1994 World Cup in America offered Montezemolo the top job. It was an open acknowledgment of Italy's expertise in running the biggest sporting event in the world. The World Cup now had an invisible stamp on the base of the trophy that read "Made in Italy." It is interesting to note that this new mythology was not deliberate propaganda but the inevitable consequence of the media's quest to provide context and meaning for its global audience.

For example, as a theme tune for its coverage of Italia '90, BBC TV chose Luciano Pavarotti's interpretation of the operatic aria "Nessun Dorma." This poignant piece was played regularly over emotionally charged, slow-motion sequences. While one of the world's most famous opera singers evoked human help-lessness in the face of destiny, BBC TV showed the world's most famous footballers falling to the ground, writhing in pain, leaping in ecstasy, screaming at each other in anger and frustration, kissing and hugging each other in celebration of a goal, or being consoled as they wept openly in defeat. By mixing elements of high culture (opera) with low culture (football), such TV montages dissimulated the economic realities of Italia '90 and focused instead on the World Cup competition as a profound and timeless pageant of human drama, full of joy, passion, and tragedy—exactly the kind of universal but essentially depoliticized qualities that sponsors prefer. The BBC's montage was so successful that for the opening ceremony of USA '94 in Los Angeles, the world-famous Three Tenors—Pavarotti, Domingo, and Carreras—sang "Nessun Dorma" again, and it has since become a sort of unofficial World Cup theme.

Another consequence of Italia '90 was that Italian *calcio* finally gained respect among British fans and players alike—who belatedly recognized that the enforced absence of English teams from European competition (they had been banned after the Heysel tragedy in 1985) had led to an enormous gulf in terms of technique and tactical awareness. England's star midfielder David Platt was the first English player to sign with an Italian club following Italia '90 and had an exceptional season with Bari before moving to Juventus. Platt was soon followed by Paul Gascoigne, who signed with Lazio, and Paul Ince with Inter Milan. The best British players realized how much they could learn from Italian football, a game that was technically and mentally more demanding than theirs—and also better paid.

However, Italy's attempts to renew its image, to recast itself as a modern, dynamic, young country—a yuppie nation, if you like—were neatly counterbalanced by the emergence during Italia '90 of Salvatore Schillaci. "The emergence of the Sicilian Schillaci in a top Northern club (Juventus) had an important impact on the north-south divide in Italy," according to Pierre Lanfranchi. "[He revived] the memory of the first economic miracle which in the 50s and 60s had fuelled a massive transfer of workers from the rural south into northern urban factories." From the 1930s on, *la vecchia signora* (the old lady) of Juventus, directed by the Fiat-owning Agnelli family, had exemplified the strong link between industry and *calcio*. Rather than representing the city of Turin (which has its own regional team, Torino),

Juventus had always represented all of Italy, its team traditionally composed of players from all over the country.

Totò Schillaci, born in a poor Palermo neighborhood, epitomized the ranks of Juventus fans who had moved north in search of work. His life story mirrored theirs and gave them hope, all the more so because, unlike the glamorous, middle-class players around him, Schillaci had made his Serie A debut only twelve months before the World Cup.

He had literally sprung from obscurity into one of Italy's top three teams, and from there into football's biggest tournament. "Schillaci's exploits," says Lanfranchi, "and the enthusiasm they generated among the fans served to reconcile a large number of Italians with their past." That he ended the competition as its highest scorer was somehow fitting, a timely reminder of a very real working-class tradition in a country that had played down its more humble and prosaic roots.

As for hooligans, Italians are perhaps lucky that their "ultras" are partisan about local teams, regional rivalries, and internal feuds between north and south, rich and poor, rather than nationalistic issues. At the very least the Italian team is not followed around the world (as the England team is) by violent thugs who attack the locals in order to prove their patriotic nature. In general, the Italian fault line runs between those who perceive themselves as the hard-working northerners and the supposedly lazy southerners that they believe they subsidize. Despite or because of this, *calcio* has little of the inverted class snobbery found in the English game and attracts an astonishingly wide spectrum of Italian society to big matches.

I have sat alongside elderly ladies in fur coats, at the top of the unfinished San Siro stadium, as we watched AC Milan trounce Como 4–0 in dense fog.

It was at the same stadium a little later that a banner appeared bearing the slogan "The Momentary Lapse of Reason." This banner was beautifully made in a funereal style—gold gothic capitals professionally printed on a black background—and huge, more than thirty feet long. But its most disturbing quality was that it was in a foreign language: English. Clearly, the fans who had fabricated it and draped it over the edge of the concrete rampart were no longer traditional hooligans, limited to chaotic and random violence, but a new kind of destructive force. They were self-aware and toying with the notion of football hooliganism as a particularly English form of violence, an imported style of mindless rage.

The fact that the phrase comes from a Pink Floyd song does not seem to make it any less menacing. We can all accept, to an extent, the idea of inarticulate louts on a drunken rampage. But there is something chilling about fanatics capable of articulating their own hysteria with such sardonic eloquence. To understand the sublime weirdness of this phenomenon, one must try and imagine its equivalent: a banner citing Umberto Eco, perhaps in faultless Italian, appearing at Anfield, Highbury, or Old Trafford. Only a moment's reflection is needed to realize that it simply could not happen. Even on the terraces, it seems, the Italian football experience has long since surpassed all others, attaining a transcendent, somewhat surreal level of sophistication and passion.

The Homemade Italian Bestseller

Fausto Colombo

Kathleen Gilje, "Portrait of a young man, restored,"

oil on canvas, 1995

(Courtesy Gorney Bravin Post Lee, New York)

In 1980, a likable and intelligent Italian professor of semiotics, known for his boundless erudition and for his skill at telling jokes and writing dazzling newspaper articles, wrote a book that was meant as little more than a divertissement—set in the Middle Ages and salted with more-or-less hidden references to the philosophies and linguistics of the period. His usual publisher printed the usual number of copies. His friends, his fans, and his acquaintances (students, colleagues, journalists) all read it—nothing new or surprising. Then something happened. The first few editions sold out rapidly. A surprising publishing phenomenon began to unfold, and the book was published in various editions throughout the world, from France to the United States; a few years later, the French director Jean-Jacques Annaud made the book into a movie. The book in question, of course, was Umberto Eco's *The Name of the Rose*.

The book's popularity—which was truly spectacular—amazed the critics. In effect, the array of half-hidden quotations and the numerous allusions to a body of knowledge meant for initiates were the sort of things that ought to discourage (everyone thought) the larger public. Yet the main reason for the book's success lay in the fact that it could be read on a number of different levels—it was a thriller, a genre that by its nature is suited to mass consumption; it had a love story; and there were even courtroom scenes (the Inquisition). And the book had all the classic elements of the light fiction that is serialized in newspapers and magazines—right down to the villainous and vindictive monks. This lowbrow warp—so to speak—was interwoven with a highbrow weft of learned references (characters who were clearly William of Ockham and Jorge Luis Borges, for instance, or quotes from abstruse texts), but it allowed the reader to look at the work from a number of different points of view. Moreover, the atmosphere of refined erudition that the pages exuded flavored the narra-

164

tive, even for a common reader, giving the impression of taking part in a high-level discussion and assuaging the inevitable sense of guilt that preys on anyone who reads a book just for fun.

Among the many ongoing discussions that were triggered by the success of *The Name of the Rose*, one in particular had to do with a generalized amazement at the idea of an Italian bestseller conquering the American public (among others), while the situation is usually the reverse. This propensity was typical of the Italian intellectual community: the Bel Paese was considered an exporter of high art and an importer of low art—mass culture. I believe that this view is profoundly false; I will set the stage with an interesting little adventure story, that of the birth of the Italian cultural industry.

Once Upon a Time

When Italy, at the end of the Risorgimento, finally attained its hard-won unity, the market for the publishing industry looked promising only to the most optimistic entrepreneurs. In 1861, one statistical survey cited a figure of seventeen million illiterates in Italy, bad news for a medium such as the book (the only medium at the time) that demands, as a minimum threshold of access, the ability to read. All the same, the culture industry found its footing, not by seeking out a mass audience but rather by focusing on a target audience. These targets were selected, in some cases, on the basis of previous consumption; thus Emilio Salgari narrated the adventures of the pirates of Malaysia and his various corsair and buccaneer heroes in a language that was familiar to readers of travel magazines and fans of the opera, and Carolina Invernizio built her feuilletons with one eye on the scandal sheets of the period. In other cases, it was a specific local situation that

Sean Connery in The Name of the Rose,

directed by Jean-Jacques Annaud, 1987

(Farabolafoto)

suggested the style and the themes to be narrated. Francesco Mastriani, for instance, constructed great serialized novels set against the background of his hometown of Naples, teeming with brigands and members of the Camorra, or Neapolitan Mafia, clearly targeting his fellow Neapolitans as his prime readership. In other cases, a certain reader was targeted, characterized either by gender or age group. This is true of women's literature (again, Invernizio is a remarkable example) or children's literature, which for nearly three decades produced memorable works that enjoyed great success outside of Italy as well: *The Adventures of Pinocchio* (1882) by Carlo Collodi (the nom de plume of Carlo Lorenzini), *Cuore* (1886) by Edmondo de Amicis, and *Il Giornalino di Gian Burrasca* (1912) by Vamba (the nom de plume of Luigi Bertelli). These three works are linked not only by a sort of invisible thematic thread but also by an almost Darwinian evolution represented in the

165

three figures of their authors. Let us begin by exploring the themes of the three works—school is the main recurring motif. The puppet Pinocchio constantly tries to escape from school, and then finally returns to school in an attempt (successful, in the end) to become a real little boy; the schoolroom is the main setting of *Cuore*, a child's diary in which the protagonist tells of the everyday life of his fellow students; and boarding school was the obsessive nightmare of the very badly behaved Gian Burrasca, as well as the setting of several of his adventures.

As for the mutation of the figure of the Italian author, Collodi emerged from the experience of the Risorgimento as a skilled printer, theater critic, public servant, translator of French fables, and, above all, author of textbooks. Success came upon him unexpectedly, from a book that became a universal classic, a book that he himself dismissed as "infantile." De Amicis, on the other hand, was already in the employ of Treves, a major publisher who sent him around Europe as a reporter. Together, the publisher and the author constructed, practically in a test tube, a proper bestseller—inspired by a novel by Michelet, *L'Amour*—that was launched in Italian bookstores on the first day of school and promoted extensively through lobbying schoolteachers. While Collodi was, all things considered, an author in the old style, parachuted into modernity, as it were, de Amicis was already a modern author in every sense of the word. *Modernissimo*—exceedingly modern—is the way we should describe Vamba, who published the *Giornalino della Domenica*, one of the very first Italian children's magazines, during the years that Italy was importing comic books from the United States and Great Britain; but Vamba made his magazine an educational tool for middle-class children, rather than a working-class, adult vehicle.

And yet, one might well object, don't these

Clint Eastwood in For a Few Dollars More,

directed by Sergio Leone, 1965

A paradigm of the spaghetti Western.

(Farabolafoto)

three stories demonstrate the opposite of what they were proffered to demonstrate? Where, in all this, do we find the worldliness of Italian culture? Rather, do these stories not simply demonstrate a continued tendency to import models from outside Italy? To respond, we must explore certain details more closely. Let us begin by observing that the way that Italy looked at the world at the end of the nineteenth century and the beginning of the twentieth century was slightly schizophrenic, swinging from the nostalgic pride of a people who perceived themselves as the heirs to a great if somewhat tattered

tradition (feelings that Italian Fascism would develop and exploit ruthlessly) to the awareness of a present in which the rest of the world—and especially the Americas—was the destination of a massive migration of the poor and, in some cases, of the desperately poverty stricken.

It is no accident that sweet old Geppetto, searching in vain for Pinocchio, makes a last, desperate attempt and builds a boat "to cross the Ocean"; and again it is no accident that *Cuore* contains perhaps the first great tale of emigration, "From the Apennines to the Andes," in which the social conscience of de Amicis merges with his sly sentimentalism. Italian emigrants—we should remember—also constituted a large market, and many Italian publishers attempted to exploit that market, in some cases succeeding. For instance, it may be worth noting that the first American editions of *Pinocchio* in English (1909 and 1911) were followed by a version in Italian (1932, published by D. C. Heath of Boston, "with notes, exercises and vocabulary by Emilio Goggio"). Migration, however, was to be the destiny of the very works we are discussing. To focus on *Pinocchio*, for instance, we need only recall that one of its successful sequels— *Il Segreto di Pinocchio*, by Gemma Rembadi Mongiardini (1894)—enjoyed an American edition with the title of *Pinocchio under the Sea* (1913). The identities of the two novels must have mingled considerably in the imaginations of the readers. Is it unreasonable to venture that the Disney screenplay (the film version of *Pinocchio* dates from 1939) was guided by a fusion of themes and episodes from the original Collodi text and its—shall we say—apocryphal continuation? Could this not explain the introduction in the cartoon version of Pinocchio's long walk on the seabed, entirely absent from Collodi's original story?

Craftsmanship and the Culture Industry: The Italian Formula

In reality, then, the Italian publishing industry at the end of the nineteenth century and the beginning of the twentieth century produced a series of products that clearly proved capable of making extensive and formidable inroads into other cultures and other territories that were more developed in industrial terms. If we wish to understand how this was possible, we must realize that the early phases of the international culture industry contained a number of potential developments, only certain of which came about and stabilized into concrete structures. In that early phase, however, Italian literary craftsmanship was one of the potential forms of mass-market standardization of cultural processes. The same can be said, after all, of the nineteenth-century Italian *canzone*, or popular song, both in its Neapolitan version and in the version that derived more explicitly from the high-art form of opera. Enrico Caruso, the celebrated tenor, an authentic star in the American market, is one example of this strong compatibility. And the Italian movie industry—which in the second decade of the twentieth century, prior to the catastrophe of World War I (let us say, until *Cabiria*), exported its products around the world—offers yet another precious example. What is the model of production of this crafts-based industry? Let us say, in somewhat simplistic terms, that its prime characteristic lies in a shared sensibility linking author and readership. Perhaps, we should say that the author is a member of his or her own readers, in the sense that he or she writes (or directs, or draws, or records) exactly what he or she would like to read (or watch, or listen to). This body of work is not based on external processes of analysis and exploration (surveys, the construction of routines based on previous successes, and so on), but on a cultural empathy.

James Coburn in Duck, You Sucker!,

directed by Sergio Leone, 1971

I have already noted that this phenomenon can be seen in Mastriani, a Neapolitan who was writing for his fellow Neapolitans; in Salgari, a passionate lover of travel, immobilized in Italy, writing exotic novels for other Italians who were never to leave the peninsula; in Invernizio, a woman writing for other women like her. This matter may seem less clear for children's literature. But here we are talking about an entire society that has a certain idea of childhood, an idea that is so powerful and so universally shared in the world of adults that it constitutes an amniotic fluid for real children. And in any case—in the work of de Amicis and Vamba—we find an adult working to create children's diaries, pretending to be a child. If Mohammed won't go to the mountain . . . In accordance with this fairly emphatic attitude, the derivation of genres from outside Italy hardly interferes with the autarkic development of styles and themes. Let us consider two absolutely fundamental examples: the first is the Italian version of Disney, the second is Sergio Leone.

The way in which Mickey Mouse came to Italy is remarkable. A smart Florentine publisher, Giuseppe Nerbini, witnessed a showing of a Mickey Mouse cartoon. It made a big impression on him. And so he founded a comic book entitled *Topolino* (to this day,

Mickey Mouse is known in Italy as Topolino). The mouse was drawn by a skillful Italian illustrator, Giove Toppi. Disney brought a lawsuit, and during the legal proceedings the comic book continued publication under the modified name of *Topo Lino*, literally, Linus the Mouse. Finally, when an agreement was reached between Nerbini and Disney, the comic book resumed publication under its original name. It was later sold to Mondadori, which immediately assembled an Italian team of illustrators and writers. In the years just before and just after World War II, the stories written and drawn in Italy were numerous and very good. The leading writers of these two periods were, respectively, Federico Pedrocchi and Guido Martina. Martina, in particular, holds the credit for creating the first Disney parody, *L'Inferno di Topolino*, inspired freely by no less than *The Divine Comedy* of Dante Alighieri. The Italian Disney characters had neither the depth of Mickey as created by Floy Gottfriedson nor the skillful epic feel of the ducks created by Carl Barks, but the school of illustrators assembled by Mondadori began an Italian "way" of Disney that even today plays a sizable role in the world production of the colossus of Burbank. Many new characters actually originated in Italy, and the tradition of the parodies was embellished with dozens of Italian stories. As for Sergio Leone, his renowned reinterpretation of the Western—with movies like *A Fistful of Dollars* (1964), *For a Few Dollars More* (1965), and *Duck, You Sucker!*, also known as *A Fistful of Dynamite* (1972), and so on—marked a turning point for the American Western, nicely embodied in the movies of Clint Eastwood, who was, in fact, the star of many of Leone's most successful films.

In these two cases, Italy's cultural craftsmanship borrowed and absorbed from America, creating a series of new and original products. The for-

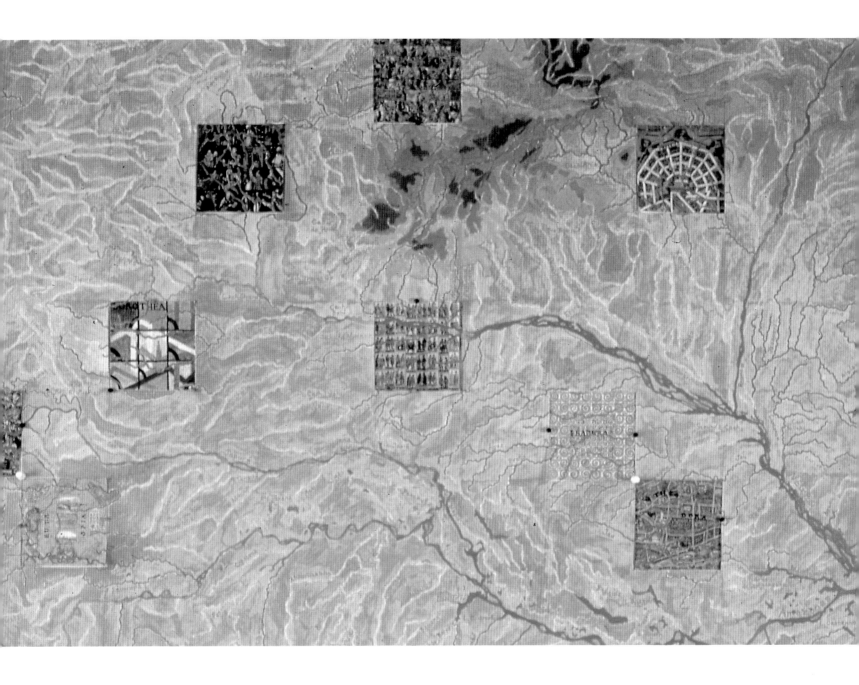

mula is the same as always. Disney's Italian writers and illustrators thought and worked in terms of the Italian audience, whose tastes they profoundly shared. Sergio Leone reinterpreted the Western (previously reinterpreted, but also placed in a new setting, by Akira Kurosawa) in a more cynical and disillusioned context, certainly more appropriate to a country like Italy, which had absorbed the Western and could not witness the melancholy decline of the cowboy. In this rewriting, however, aimed at a clearly defined national audience, often with exceedingly precise characteristics, the story was designed and implemented by the cultural craftsman with

an awareness of the potential of medium and means (which might well be exceedingly limited) against a cultural background that was anything but provincial, indeed, open to a mass readership, a global marketplace. And that is why many Italian creations have sold outside Italy, and especially in America—the audiences of the entire world, when viewed from within, from the beating heart of their emotions, resemble each other much more than they do if viewed from without, through the lenses of marketing and statistics. In *Postille a Il Nome della Rosa* (*An Afterword to The Name of the Rose*), Umberto Eco (who is, among other things, one of the

leading scholars of mass culture in Italy) wrote: "I wanted the reader to have fun. At least as much fun as I was having." Here, the learned professor, author of a novel full of obscure references intended for a narrow circle of friends, has identified and revived once again the formula for the international success of so many Italian products. An old story has started up again—and no one can say it ever ended.

Italian Holidays

Carlo Tombola

There can be no question about Italy's success as a world tourist attraction. Interwoven in that success are the fundamental qualities and the various events of recent economic development, along with a series of changes in mindset and perception of the space in which we live. First and foremost, however, the leading factor contributing to that success has been the popularity of the image of Italy outside of Italy; that image has had effects whose importance lies not so much in the numbers (which, as we shall see, are impressive enough on their own) as in the way that it contributed in a decisive manner to the formation and consolidation of the overall image of the country in the eyes of its own inhabitants: a reflected image. As Cesare De Seta has pointed out, it was above all non-Italian travelers who kept alive an ideal conception of a united Italy in the long centuries of the peninsula's political fragmentation, a role not unlike that of the great men of letters—from Dante to Alessandro Manzoni—who laid the foundations of an Italian cultural tradition, who conceived of an Italian nation long before it was possible to speak of an Italian state.

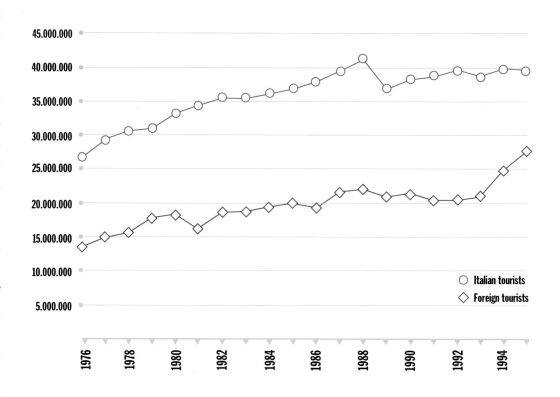

Image from a tourist brochure,

1950s

(Publifoto Olympia)

Statistics concerning flow of tourists, which seem to show that in the last forty years the boom in non-Italian tourism in Italy has been greatly outweighed by the growth in domestic Italian tourism, can be deceiving. It is true, admittedly, that the weight of domestic tourism (constituted by Italian residents on holiday inside Italy) is greater than that of inbound tourism (non-Italian visitors coming to Italy) and that of outbound tourism (Italian citizens who choose to travel outside Italy). All the same, of the 68 million tourists counted in 1995 (counted because they availed themselves of commercial tourist services), no fewer than 28 million came to Italy from abroad, and there has been a notable increase in their numbers over recent years (up by 60 percent between 1988 and 1995); moreover,

these non-Italian tourists accounted for 40 percent of the visitors to Italy's hospitality structures—providing an annual contribution of 45 to 50 trillion lire (roughly 30 billion dollars) to the Italian balance of trade.

On the other hand, the flow of Italian tourism inside Italy, following a constant rate of growth throughout the 1970s and much of the 1980s, and the decline registered in 1989 and 1990, has stabilized at levels of 38 to 39 million people annually. Clearly, this flow is much more sensitive to the state of the Italian economy and its effects on Italian families and their disposable income, as opposed to the popularity of the image of Italy as a tourist destination among potential vacationers residing in Italy. Which is to say, within Italy as well, the success of

171

Festa di San Paolo, Palazzolo Acreide, Sicily

Photograph by Marie Louise Brimberg from National Geographic

Opposite:

Dolomites, Italy

Autochrome Rogers Collection,

National Geographic Society

tourism as a whole is tied, first and foremost, to profound changes in general social and economic conditions, such as, for example, a rise in incomes and a widening of the right to holidays. Those conditions are common to all residents of the wealthy West: according to a recent survey, more than half the population of Italy enjoys one or more periods a year of vacation, with an annual average of twenty-one days, in line with the European average.

The most notable feature of Italy lies in the unusual development of its tourist image, which has benefited not only from the unique mix of a vast historical and cultural heritage and a lovely landscape but also from a tourist profile that differs from all other leading countries in world tourism, even though Italy is equipped with a far less impressive organizational and professional structure than countries with a solid tradition in the hospitality industry, such as the United States and France, and is less dependent on the beachside facilities of the leading countries in the inbound tourism category, such as Spain and Greece, or the tropical archipelagoes of various developing nations.

Let us leave aside, in this analysis, the long period of incubation of Italy's tourist image, which—according to De Seta—originated in the sixteenth century or even earlier along the main routes of the medieval religious pilgrimage toward Rome, the city of Saint Peter. Our treatment will be limited to the years that were decisive in the formation of a mass image, which may be identified—as is the case with many of the most salient changes in Italian society and the territory of Italy—as between the late 1960s and the early 1970s. In that crucial moment of transition, most of the quality tourist sites had already been discovered and exploited by non-Italian travelers, in some cases dating back as far as the Grand Tour; they were scattered throughout the various

regions of Italy and included all of the main typologies: in the so-called cities of art and culture, around the various archaeological sites, at the various thermal spas, at the base of the most important massifs of the Alps, along the shores at various resorts, and on the larger and smaller islands.

The first resort centers, and with them the networks of seasonal professions and related services, had already been established and consolidated, often as a result of the prestige and renown won among various non-Italian visitors, whose numbers were now growing in direct proportion to average disposable income. It was then, specifically beginning in the mid-1970s, that most of the territory of Italy was touched by the King Midas of mass tourism, Italian style, with a proliferation of cement and speculative construction that actually distorted and, in some cases, virtually destroyed the attractions that had allowed it to prosper. This tourist industry, on the other hand, was also flexible and tireless in encouraging or resisting long-term social and economic processes, such as the deruralization of the hill and foothill country (consider, in this connection, the range of the Ligurian Apennines, from Ventimiglia to La Spezia) or the depopulation of the middle and higher Alpine valleys; it was also capable of creating employment—part-time, short-term, or minimum-wage, admittedly—in areas of dying industries, from the steel mills and mines of the Val d'Aosta and Elba to the shipbuilding of the Tyrrhenian and Adriatic coasts.

Although serious research on the subject still needs to be done, the phenomenon of the second home—though full of gray areas and difficult to quantify—has been the product especially of real-estate purchases on the part of the upper classes, and later the middle classes, of the large metropolitan areas of northern and central Italy, but it has also involved considerable numbers of French, Swiss, and German habitués, without reaching the peaks of the massive Germanization seen later in Spain (on the Costa Brava and the Balearic Islands)—not even on Elba. Increased by the more permanent currents of those with second homes in Italy, the flow of non-Italian visitors acquired—in that short period of time—its basic characteristics and seasonal rhythms, and selected the various prime destinations and the means of travel, taking on, despite the unquestionable inadequacy of the system of accommodations, the profile that is recognizable even today, some twenty-five to thirty years from its beginning.

In this sense, the growing popularity and success of the various Italian tourist basins was primarily a result of the new geographic accessibility of the various attractions and was decisively bound up with the improvement in land transportation of continental Europe. It is, therefore, a result, and not a secondary result, of the mass market for automobiles, punctuated by the construction of the main sections of the network of superhighways: the inauguration of the Milan-Florence superhighway (1962); the Florence-Rome superhighway (1964); the Mont Blanc Tunnel (1965); the Ventimiglia-La Spezia superhighway (1971); the Modena-Brenner superhighway (to the Brenner Pass); the Autostrada della Cisa, a superhighway from the north to western Tuscany (1972); and so on. The spread of the automobile completely overshadowed the memory of the heroic years, during the first boom of tourism in Italy, between the end of the nineteenth century and the first years of the twentieth century, in conjunction with the linkage of Italy to the rail network of continental Europe through the new Alpine tunnels: years in which a train called the Valigia delle Indie, or Suitcase of the Indies, ran from Modane to Brindisi through the Col de Fréjus via the Mont Cenis Tunnel (inaugurated in 1871), while the Saint Gotthard Tunnel (1882) was called, in a somewhat rhetorical flourish, "La Via delle Genti," literally, the Way of the Peoples.

Nor, in more recent years, have the new and profitable market niches (such as Japanese tourism

Opposite:

Evening traffic, Palermo

Photograph by H. Brooks Walker

from National Geographic

and conference tourism, weekend tour packages, intermodal airplane-and-cruise, or airplane-and-coach packages, and so on) been established just because the sharp drop in airfares truly modified the geography of non-Italian tourism as it first took shape about thirty years ago. Nowadays, most visitors to Italy enter the country over the land borders (four out of five, to be exact), and it would almost seem irrelevant to think of Italy's onetime maritime gates to the world, considering that only 3.5 percent of all arrivals enter by seaports: yet another demonstration of the degree to which geographic destiny is constantly undermined by the organized activities of humankind.

The predilection of non-Italians for a private means of transportation, like the automobile, which is flexible and well-suited for short to medium distances, helps to explain such questions as why the province of Bolzano is the Italian province that ranks second in number of non-Italian visitors (closely trailing Venice) and ranks first far-and-away in terms of accommodations (almost 150,000 beds; after the third-ranked province of Rimini, the fourth ranking goes to the province of Trento). On the whole, the great river of tourists (and tourist money) that flows into Italy from abroad goes—almost exclusively—to the regions of central and northern Italy, with the enclave of Naples and its surrounding area also being a popular destination.

The same criterion of accessibility is useful in drawing a map of the provenance of non-Italian tourists. Clearly, there is a prevalence of tourists from the European Union (60 percent): it couldn't have been otherwise, because the tourist leadership of western Europe, which receives two-thirds of all international tourism every year, is the fundamental core of the world tourist industry, a sector—now mature—that generates an annual turnover of 320 to 330 billion dollars, growing constantly over the

past fifty years. Leading the ranking are German tourists (29 percent), followed by the French (8 percent), the British (6 percent), and the Austrians (5.5 percent). From outside of the European Union come the Americans (10 percent), the Japanese (7 percent), and the Swiss (4.5 percent). The longest stays are those of tourists from the monetary area of the German mark (five to six days on average) with a gradual tendency to grow shorter, which seems to be a physiological feature in all the sectors of the mass vacation industry.

As for the seasonal progression, it has its peak in July (13 percent) with only slight declines in the other months from May to September, in contrast to domestic Italian tourism, where the number of travelers in August is double that of September. Behavior differs by nationality: the Germans prefer May and August, the Americans tend to avoid the crowding of August but extend the season right up to October, and the arrivals from Japan are constant throughout the year (which has an extremely posi-

tive effect on the occupancy rates of the major hotels) with a clear preference for the month of March, when Japan celebrates the vernal equinox. Finally, the geography of tourist attractions is far more complex than might appear from raw statistical data. In general, non-Italians come to Italy to tour the cities of historic and artistic interest (40 percent), though on shorter stays (two to three nights) than tourists visiting seaside resorts (five to six nights on average) or lakeside resorts (four to five nights). A first, moderate surprise comes from the popularity of sites around the great sub-Alpine lakes, which seem to be much less popular with domestic Italian tourists (though there the considerable number of second homes is surely shaping the statistics).

It should come as no surprise to learn of the considerable share of non-Italians who avoid the hotels of the city and turn to the network of non-hotel accommodations: for instance, campsites, tourist villages, private but "registered" accommodations, so-called agri-tourism facilities, hostels,

mountain huts—this is a choice made by a comparable sector of non-Italians and Italians (15 percent non-Italians as compared to 13.5 percent Italians), preferred in particular by Germans, Dutch, and Austrians, as well as by the less well-to-do tourists from eastern Europe.

The greatest proportional presence in the high-end hotels (four and five stars, and five stars deluxe) is once again constituted by Germans (26 percent) and Britons (9 percent) and, from outside of the European Union, Americans (13 percent) and Japanese (11 percent). This is the tourist circuit that commands the big money, where the proportion of non-Italian visitors is highest (56 percent). In Italy, this circuit comprises about a hundred hotels, which constitute the stronghold of the roughly two hundred hotels owned by chains. Solidly placed in the international reservations systems, capable of offering attractive packages of additional combinations (monument tours, guided shopping, evenings at the theater, secretaries for conferences, etc.), and with elevated standards of hospitality, the luxury hotels are concentrated in the big cities (ten in Rome, eight in Florence, six in Milan, three in Venice) and in the most prestigious elite tourist resorts: along the Amalfi coast, on Capri, in the spa region of the Euganean Hills, and on Lake Garda.

In order to complete our survey of the map of Italian tourism, we should add the most popular districts of mass tourism: aside from those mentioned above in Alto Adige and Trentino, we should include the Adriatic coastline from Jesolo to Fano, the largest Lombard lakes, the coastline around Savona, the area known as Versilia, and the various routes linked to the memory of Saint Francis in Umbria. The rest lie in a nebula of small areas specializing in winter sports along the entire Alpine arc and in the central Apennines, or else in the beach resorts—often linked one to another like a long chain—along the entire coastline of the Italian boot and its many islands. The Osservatorio Turistico Nazionale delle Città d'Arte (literally, National Observatory on Tourism in the Art Capitals) estimates that 309 Italian townships (out of 8,000) account for the bulk of the Italian national tourist system. All the same, the distinctive feature of Italian tourism—in economic reality and in the image that is reflected from that reality—is the ubiquitous role of the city, or perhaps we should say, the network of small, mid-size, and large cities that, in terms of the scale of European and American history, could all be classified as historical centers. This network has for centuries been fundamental to the urban fabric of central and northern Italy, while also informing the organization of the countryside; in addition, it contains an unrivaled array of residential typologies, set within a rich framework of agrarian landscapes, detectable here and there in their traditional forms, in combinations that constitute a deposit of tourist resources still awaiting discovery and exploitation.

Let us add another powerful factor. This same dense urban network corresponds to the network of the industrial districts, a network that has successfully exported the image of Italian manufacturing (known in Italy as "Made in Italy") throughout the world. The geographic proximity of manufacturing districts and tourist attractions, besides increasing local employment opportunities, has worked as a flywheel both for the popularity outside Italy of Italian products—through the spontaneous mediation of the non-Italian tourist—and for providing a further reason for coming to Italy (shopping) alongside cultural reasons or the desire for relaxation and fun. It is therefore no accident that Italy's manufacturing success should be that much greater in the areas of consumption that we can describe as the three Fs (food, fashion, and furniture), closely bound up not only with the manufacturing experience of the districts but also with the tastes and lifestyle of the Italians.

We may still ask to what degree all these various factors contributed to the overall success and popularity of the image of Italy outside of Italy. A specific response comes from an Italian government agency, the Department of Tourism, which recently undertook two surveys concerning the image of Italy, both among potential visitors and among nonspecialized journalists in fourteen countries (Argentina, Austria, Belgium, Canada, China, England, France, Germany, Holland, Japan, Poland, Russia, Spain, and the United States).

It is a response that reiterates the power of the stereotypes of historic memory, leaving in the background the issues of politics and sports presented by the mass media. In response to the question "What have you heard about Italy?," the most common spontaneous answers had to do with Italy as a vacation spot and as a treasure trove of culture, art, and entertainment; followed, respectively, by sporting events, considerations related to religion and the Pope, organized crime, politics, fine food, and climate. In a report card on the image of Italy among non-Italians, the best grades are given, in declining order, to culture and art, to Italy as a vacation spot, to the quality of the wine, and to the quality of Italian products. After the experience of a trip to Italy, the grades generally rise—indicator of an overall favorable impression and the desire to return—with the highest praise going to art capitals and great artworks, the landscape and the natural environment, the cuisine, the hospitality and friendliness of the Italians, the wine, and the quality and variety of the products available in stores. Among the interviewees, the cool evaluations offered by the English and the Germans improved considerably; the most enthusiastic—before and after—remained the Russians and the Argentines, while among the Asians (Chinese and Japanese) there was a sense of disappointment.

What can we conclude? That non-Italians are coming to Italy in search of a confirmation of the traditional stereotypes, that is, the Tower of Pisa and the Dolomites; Armani and the Pope; pizza, spaghetti, and wine? The answer to that is yes; nobody—not even a hurried visitor—likes being disappointed, and stereotypes become even more deeply rooted when it is possible to buy physical records of them, such as souvenirs (cheaply, as has been the case to date). So part of the Italian success story consists of having rendered physical and material—for a profit—something that originally had no economic category. But if we look too closely at the present-day reality of the Italian landscape, Italian style, Italian hospitality, and the extensive deterioration of the Italian natural environment and social structure, we begin to suspect that all this is a product of a one-way love on the part of the peoples of northern Europe for Italy, the Land of Sunshine: a love that is not particularly interested in reflecting (upon) the image of the actual country.

Sections of the Italian landscape,
Venice Biennale, 1997
1. From Florence toward Pistoia
2, 3. From Milan toward Como
Photograph by Gabriele Basilico

Rome

Photograph by D. Cleek

(Grazia Neri)

Rome

Photograph by D. Cleek

(Grazia Neri)

177

Valuing the Italian Dream

Andrea Balestri   Marco Ricchetti

A people of poets, artists, heroes, saints, thinkers, scientists, navigators, and transmigrators.

Palace of Italian Civilization—EUR, Rome

The "Italian-ness" of Italian Exports

What most helps to shape the image of Italy around the world? The artistic heritage? The cuisine? Certain collective forms of behavior—real or imagined—of the Italians? Whatever the prevailing factor, we can be sure that a certain depiction of Italy—concrete, but not necessarily true—takes shape every day in the decisions of millions of consumers around the world when they buy products that are "Made in Italy." Commercial exchanges—just like cultural fashions or fads in tourism—show what people like best about a country for reasons of cost or taste. In the early nineteenth century, the English economist David Ricardo illustrated his theory of international trade by depicting Portugal as a sunny agrarian land and a great exporter of fine wines, contrasting it with the idea of a "modern" England as a land of industry and mining, exporting manufactured fabrics at competitive prices thanks to the use of looms driven by the first steam engines. This is an example that survives today in university textbooks, not only because of the clarity and importance of Ricardo's theoretical postulation but also because of the evocative power of the images of the two nations.

Do the goods that Italy manufactures and exports contribute nowadays to the creation of an image of the Bel Paese that is just as well defined as the image created by the goods exported by Portugal or England in the early nineteenth century? And if the answer to that question is yes, what sort of image of Italy emerges from the international markets?

In order to answer the first of the two questions, we must ask whether the structure of Italian exports differs substantially from that of other nations; in other words, whether the image of Italy among consumers in the rest of the world will be increasingly sharply defined to the degree that goods exported by Italian manufacturers and businesses are significantly different from those exported by their competitors and counterparts in other nations. The answer is less obvious and banal than it might seem at first glance. In referring to England and Portugal, Ricardo clearly understood that the former was hardly a sun-kissed land, and that it did not possess the climate needed to produce port; in the same sense, it was clear that Portugal, unlike England, did not possess the necessary technological know-how to make use of the power created by steam engines. It was therefore fitting that Portugal specialize in making wine and that England specialize in spinning and weaving cotton. The pattern of trade and commerce that established an image of two such

Loading Maserati automobiles onto
an Alitalia airplane headed for Sebring,
Milan, Linate, March 10, 1961

(Publifoto Olympia)

179

Wrapping paper for "export"

oranges

(Civica Raccolta delle Stampa A. Bertarelli)

different lands was based on solid and easily measured differences. These are the same differences that today explain (just like with the fine wines of Portugal in the first half of the nineteenth century) why the three leading categories of exports for a tropical country like El Salvador should be, in order, coffee, sugarcane, and crayfish (one should note, by the way, that El Salvador is undertaking a forced march toward industrialization).

We cannot, however, look to geographic or climatic factors, substantial differences in labor costs, and a lesser or greater availability of financial capital or technological know-how in attempting to explain significant differences in the mercantile specialization of a country like Italy as compared with other nations such as France, Germany, Great Britain, Japan, and the United States, which are all quite similar in terms of degree of development, climate, and economic fundamentals. The interpretation that largely prevails among economists is that as we proceed along the path of economic development, the wave of globalization and the growing degree of economic interdependence tend to diminish the margin by which it is possible to preserve in the individual national systems specific and distinctive features of social, cultural, and economic organization. According to this line of thinking, companies in all nations will tend to adopt the same manufacturing technologies; consumer behavior will tend to be aligned in accordance with a lifestyle that is becoming standardized around the world; the globalization and sophistication of financial markets will unify macroeconomic performance. There can be no doubt that this is a case in which the predictions of a future where the diversities of national cultures will tend to disappear (as endorsed by eco-

nomic orthodoxy) fully earns economics its reputation as "the dismal science." The fact that a distinct depiction of Italy and its specific products should persist in the international marketplace, and especially the fact that there are no signals on the horizon of a substantial shift in the unmistakable "mercantile" image of the Bel Paese, tend to undercut the reliability of these predictions. Let us look at the numbers to find how different the goods that Italy exports are from those that other industrialized nations export. If we compare the index of resemblance (the Grubel-Lloyd index) of the export structure for each of the leading industrialized nations to each of the other five, we find that in most cases Italy can be seen to have a distinctly mercantile vocation.

This intricate interplay of bilateral comparison is depicted in the graph in Table 1. The meaning of this sort of spiderweb is as follows: each country is represented by a line; Italy is the red line. The line representing each country intersects the axis of each of the other five countries at the tips of the spiderweb; the closer the line of each country—where it meets the axis of the country with which it is being compared—is to the external border, the more closely their exports resemble each other in terms of type and structure. In the graph, of course, every country resembles itself perfectly; thus, Italy's red line touches the external border exactly at the axis of Italy. The red line, however, is farthest from the external border where it intersects the axes of the United States, Germany, and Japan. This means that Italy—in the group of the leading economies—possesses an export structure that differs most from that of the United States, Germany, and Japan. Italy shows a greater affinity with France and the United Kingdom; the differ-

1.
**The diamond of differences
in the structure of the exports
of the 6 leading industrialized nations**

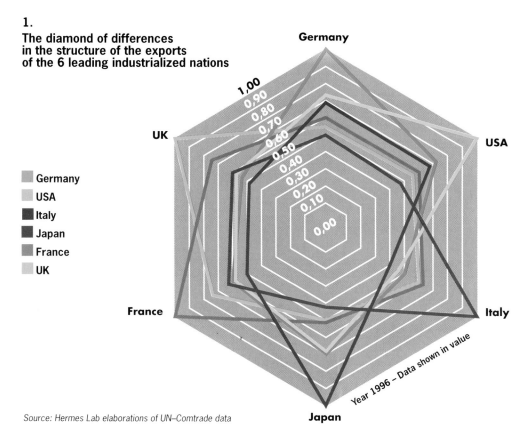

- Germany
- USA
- Italy
- Japan
- France
- UK

Source: Hermes Lab elaborations of UN–Comtrade data

ence is roughly comparable to that between the United States and Germany. In any case, Italy— followed by Japan and the United Kingdom in this intricate classification—is the nation that shows the broadest differences from other nations. Aside from the various comparisons, the network allows us in any case to answer the first question in the affirmative: Italy's exports show features that distinguish them sharply from the other leading industrialized nations.

A Postmodern Structure of Exports

Having ascertained that the structure of Italian exports presents a marked and distinctive character (Italian-ness, to be exact), it remains to be seen whether this character can be given a consistent profile that can be construed as an image of Italy, and, especially, how to determine just what image Italian goods present to the world. The remarkable exploits of Italian exports in the sector of consumer products (textiles and apparel, footwear, home furnishings, furniture, and so on), which economic theories traditionally assign to countries with lower cost factors, have attracted the interest of many researchers. A considerable

number of studies focus in particular on the backwardness (and, hence, the vulnerability) intrinsic to the structure of Italian exports, emphasizing in particular the absence of the products that form part of the world of high technology. This interpretation, in its reductive outlines (generally picturesque in its depiction), portrays Italy as a country hovering perennially somewhere between underdevelopment and modernity. The main limitation of this interpretation lies precisely in the fact that it is incapable of explaining the durable success of Italian exports, even after the consolidation of the presence on international markets of countries with decidedly lower cost factors than Italy's, countries that enjoyed enormous advantages in the production of "technologically backward" goods. More recently, an effort has been made to explain the performance of Italian exports in analytical terms that go beyond the mere content of technological innovation that can be measured by elements such as patents or formal laboratory research. For example, Marco Fortis recently took this approach in a project in which he drew persuasive new boundaries of "Made in Italy" focusing on the platform of "person-fashion-furnishings-home-food." This platform includes a series of goods that are anything but obvious, sharing a common denominator, which—no matter how you look at it—reflects (and at the same time helps to define) the "Italian way of life" in a very consistent fashion.

If we turn once again to the raw statistics on international trade, the character of "Made in Italy" emerges clearly. Out of the total exports of G7 nations, Italy accounts for just 9 percent, but if we look at certain products in the fashion system, Italy's share rises, and sharply: 66 perent for footwear, 54 percent for jewelry, 49 percent for fine fabrics, 38 percent for menswear, and so on, as shown in Table 2. The shares are not that different for the products of the home and home-furnishing industry (54 percent for tiles and building materials, 37 percent for furniture, 32 percent for lamps and lighting equipment) and the food industry (37 percent for food-processing machinery, 23 percent for fruit preserves, 22 percent for grain-based preparations—including spaghetti, Italy's leading icon).

In order to have a clear idea—in contrast—of the features that characterize Italy's mercantile image, Table 3 summarizes the same operation for Japan, whose share of G7 exports is almost twice that of Italy (18 percent). But it reaches its highest points for a series of products that are quite different in nature from their Italian counterparts: personal stereos, cameras, videotape recorders, watches, and the like. In practice, consumer choices indicate preferences (and, indirectly, images of countries) that are quite diverse: Italy leads in the manufacture of products with a high design content, bound up particularly with the person or the depiction of the person, while Japan leads in products—again, meant for individual consumption—where the technological component is particularly high.

The strength of Italian specialization can be seen in the statistics concerning per capita exports. The work done by Fortis shows, for instance, that the value of Italy's per capita exports for the system comprising "person-fashion-furnishings-home-food" were higher (1992) than German per capita exports for means of transport and Japanese per capita exports for electric and electronic devices (respectively, U.S.

2. The Image of Italy as Revealed by World Markets (1996)

Products	Italian share of G7 exports	Value of Italian Exports (in millions of U.S. $)
Total Exports	9%	27,820
Fashion system		
Footwear	66%	8,099
Leather	55%	3,066
Jewelry	54%	4,653
Woolen, silk, and linen textiles	49%	3,074
Clothing accessories	44%	2,016
Suitcases and luggage	42%	1,567
Menswear	38%	2,663
Various apparel	38%	5,519
Womenswear	34%	3,058
Cotton fabrics	27%	1,585
Women's knitwear	27%	660
Fabrics made with chemical fibers	24%	2,640
Knit fabrics	24%	764
Paints and dyes	23%	93
Threads and yarns	22%	2,575
Leather goods	20%	75
Men's knitwear	20%	258
Products for the home		
Tiles and construction materials	54%	5,764
Furniture and furnishings	37%	8,203
Lamps and lighting equipment	32%	1,263
Electric appliances	30%	5,094
Bathroom furnishings, boilers, radiators	30%	915
Crockery	24%	445
Stone, marble, and stone materials	21%	303
Valves and faucets	20%	2,704
Metal structures	20%	1,013
Food products		
Machinery for the food industry	37%	970
Fruit preserves	23%	407
Grain-based preparations	22%	1,535
Various grain-based preparations	21%	48
Fruit juices	20%	335
Non-soft vegetable oils	20%	70

Source: Hermes Lab elaborations of UN-Comtrade data

$1,1790, $1,075, and $ 903 per capita).

Tell Me What You Export and I Will Tell You Who You Are!

There are, then, perfectly good arguments supporting the idea that the goods exported by Italy are substantially different from those exported by other industrialized nations and that these goods are a set of products rich in immaterial contents, such as design and an ability to interpret the spirit of the times: threads and yarns, fabrics,

Products	Japanese share of G7 exports	Value of Japanese Exports (in millions of U.S. $)
Total exports	18%	439,032
Audio/Video recorders	72%	5,559
Photographic equipment	63%	4,421
Motorcycles and bicycles	58%	5,804
Boats and ships	58%	10,932
Radio receivers	53%	2,284
Timepieces	46%	2,238
Various optical instruments	45%	1,554
Transistors and electric valves	44%	40,847
Parts for machine tools	44%	5,099
Televisions	37%	2,256
Rolled steel-alloy sheet metal	36%	4,317
Stationery products	36%	1,265
Fiberoptics	36%	2,078
Office machinery and accessories	35%	20,290
Photographic materials	34%	4,188
Mechanical transmission equipment	33%	3,334
Steel and iron sheet metal	33%	4,485
Internal combustion engines	33%	13,119

Source: Hermes Lab elaborations of UN-Comtrade data

Products for which Italy leads the world in terms of positive trade balance:

Woolen threads and yarns
Woolen fabrics
Silk fabrics
Socks and sweaters
Ties and scarves
Eyeglasses
Gold jewelry
Cured leather
Footwear
Ornamental stones
Ceramic tiles
Chairs and sofas
Furniture and kitchen products
Lamps and lighting equipment
Faucets and valves
Ovens
Refrigerators
Washing machines
Pasta

Products for which Italy comes in second in the world in terms of positive trade balance:

Leather goods
Menswear
Womenswear
Cooking utensils and silverware
Wine

Source: Marco Fortis, Università Cattolica, Montedison

knitwear, suits, hosiery, shoes, eyeglasses, jewelry, furniture, home furnishings, and so on. All of these products, arrayed together under the rubric "Made in Italy," contribute to the definition of (and also reflect) a very specific depiction of Italy. New and more fundamental questions emerge, however, at this point. Why is Italy such a different case? And, moreover, what are the "economic fundamentals" that determine Italy's difference from the other great economies of the industrialized world?

In just a few years, with a rapidity that is reminiscent of what happened in geopolitical terms in the wake of the fall of the Berlin Wall, many economic and cultural barriers have collapsed, but unlike what orthodox economics led us to expect, the winds of globalization, instead of flattening one and all to the same configuration, have emphasized the specific qualities of various countries and, on a smaller scale, various regions. From this disparity between reality and theory begins to emerge the idea that even in a global marketplace, national

(or regional) economic systems with different characteristics can coexist, each of these systems being tied to the specific historic developments, institutions, and even images of various countries or regions.

This undermines the foundation of the interpretation whereby in a global marketplace every country (or region) resembles a little company that competes against other nation-companies that produce the same goods with their technologies. Everywhere, asymmetries of information and/or power, organizational factors, paths of development, differences in social infrastructure, economies of scale, and so on contribute to the segmentation of the global marketplace, creating a variety of differentiating factors and niches, crystallizing the specific features of each nation into images, depictions that, in turn, are transformed into further differentiating factors that tend to reinforce the niches. Which of these factors are at work in establishing Italy's specialities and images?

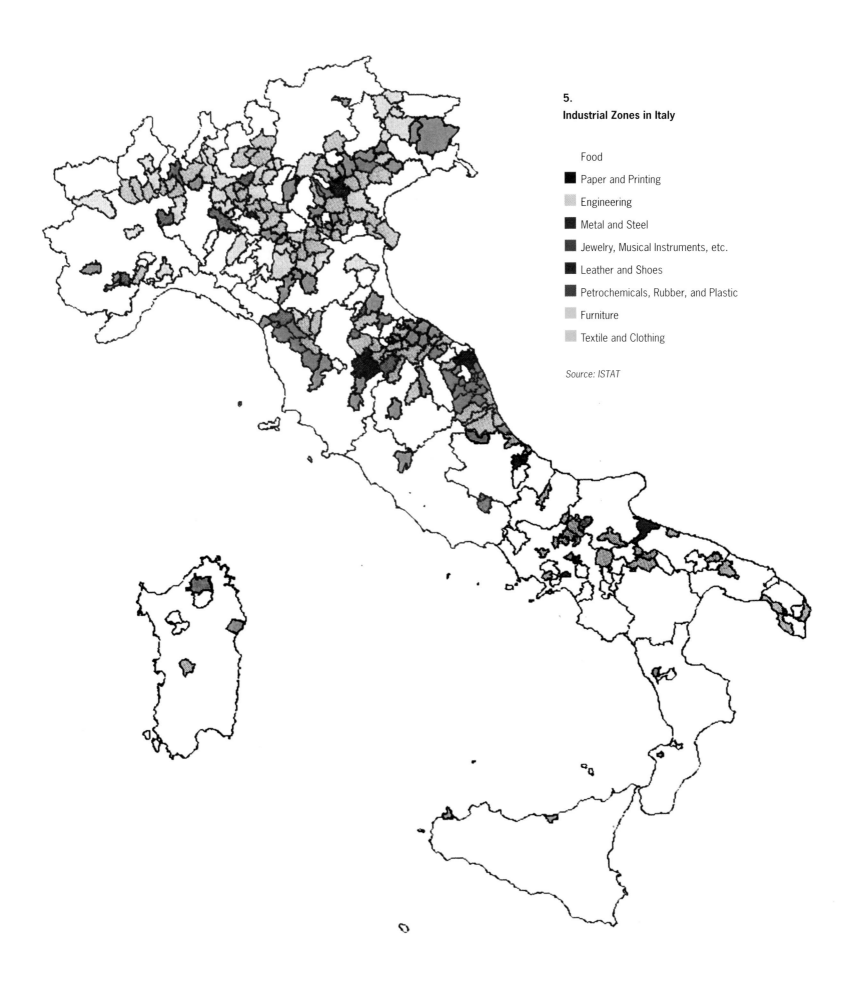

5.
Industrial Zones in Italy

Food
■ Paper and Printing
▨ Engineering
■ Metal and Steel
▨ Jewelry, Musical Instruments, etc.
■ Leather and Shoes
■ Petrochemicals, Rubber, and Plastic
▨ Furniture
▨ Textile and Clothing

Source: ISTAT

6. Share of the Italian Districts in the World Exports of Certain Products		
Product	**District**	**Share (%)**
Tiles and ceramics	Sassuolo	39.2
Silk textiles	Como	25.9
Woolen textiles	Prato	19.6
Eyeglasses	Belluno	17.6
Woolen textiles	Biella	14.0
Gold jewelry	Vicenza	14.0
Ornamental stones, marble	Carrara	13.0
Gold jewelry	Arezzo	13.0
Ornamental stones, marble	Verona	10.1
Cured leather	Arzignano	10.0
Furniture and kitchens	Alto Livenza	7.7
Sofas and chairs	Santeramo, Altamura	7.2
Sofas and chairs	Magnago	6.9
Leather	Santa Croce	6.0
Footwear	Fermo, Civitanova M.	6.0
Faucets and valves	Novara, Vercelli	5.5
Furniture and kitchens	Brianza	4.8
Cooking utensils and silverware	Lumezzane	4.1
Faucets and valves	Lumezzane	3.8
Furniture and kitchens	Pesaro	3.2

Source: Marco Fortis, Università Cattolica, Montedison

A few useful indicators in this connection can be obtained by comparing the image of Italy that emerges from its exports with several of the most commonly held images of Italy: the image of a country made up of small towns and cities dating back to the Renaissance; the image of the daring Italian sailor and explorer. Concerning Italy as a land of art treasures, the fact that Italians live in the country that boasts what may be the richest monumental heritage on earth constitutes—in the opinion of many—a collective school that develops the sense for aesthetics and fine things. But a number of specific aspects of Italian economic development in the postwar period will help to highlight the economic fundamentals of the success of what Italians call "Made in Italy" in the leading sectors in Italian exports, as well as the close ties between the original practices of Italian capitalism—a form based on family businesses, lean structures, and an atmosphere of cooperation.

The Industrial Districts

The mercantile image of Italy is closely bound up—as we shall see—with a special factor in Italy's economic development: the industrial districts. These are fairly narrow territorial systems (the largest ones have populations of about 400,000) in which there has developed over time a dense interweaving between physical life and the manufacturing activities in which the residents are involved.

Within the districts, the organization of production is based on a complex and careful division of labor among groups of small and midsize companies that benefit reciprocally from the concentration of activities belonging to the same manufacturing system in the same area. The concentration in certain regions of a great number of businesses openly competing with one another tends to stimulate innovation. In this particular climate—made up of diffuse entrepreneurial activity and unspoken rules governing economic activity, with its widespread spirit of emulation and its willingness to accept the new—Italy's small and midsize companies have developed a special skill for rapidly designing and industrializing a great array of new products, while still suc-

cessfully satisfying consumers' needs for personalization and value.

There are a great many sorts of added value associated with the organization of production by district; most of them have to do with design and style. Because of the way that they operate, the districts are reminiscent of a huge fair, in which businessmen can quickly gather a great quantity of information and compare the features and prices of various products. At the opposite extreme, the entrepreneurs of the districts—with their constant travel throughout the international marketplace—gather information directly allowing them to segment their markets and adapt their production to meet the demands of their end consumers.

As is the case for Italy as a whole, the districts also have their own mercantile image, associated with the dominant form of production that constitutes the foundation of their identity: the silk products of Como, the marble of Carrara, the women's hosiery of Castel Goffredo, the leather of Santa Croce, the woolens of Prato and Biella, the sofas of Altamura-Santeramo in Colle, the silverware and household furnishings of Omegna and Lumezzane, the jewelry of Valenza Po and Arezzo, the footwear of Fermo and the Valle del Brenta, the hiking boots of Montebelluna, the ceramics of Sassuolo.

Over the last few years, various maps of the districts and their products have been drawn up; ISTAT has identified about two hundred districts that account, overall, for some 40 percent of Italy's manufacturing employment (Table 5). The close association between these specialized centers and the mercantile image of Italy emerges even more clearly when viewed in terms of international trade: according to various sources, the share of production by the districts ranges from 30 to 50 percent. An immediate correspondence arises from a comparison of the figures shown in Table 6, concerning the specializations and shares in world exports of the leading dis-

186

tricts, with those shown in Tables 2 and 4, which depict the Italian model of specialization: the Italian image and market share are solid for those products that are the result of a solid presence inthe industrial districts.

These figures are especially impressive if we consider the fact that nearly 40 percent of the world's ceramics exports comes from Sassuolo and a few neighboring towns, or that one-quarter of the world's exports of silk products comes from a few small towns on the shores of Lake Como, or that the provinces of Biella and Prato account for nearly a quarter of the world's exports of woolens. The districts feature an intricate and well-organized world—these are towns that have best preserved the heritage of art, nature, culture, folklore, and fine cuisine that Italy has inherited from the past; at the same time, these are the towns in which it is most possible to sense the developments of the new, the desire to create and to explore the future. From this point of view, the districts are a giant reservoir of new stimuli, organized around solid good taste and a gift for original creativity. In fact, the most important sources of the mercantile image of Italy are fed by the determination and achievements of this "lesser Italy," made up primarily of small towns that have succeeded in grafting the values of modern industry onto the branch of craft tradition, with a great passion for technique and for beautiful things.

The importance of the districts is understood even outside of the mercantile milieu; for the past few years, in fact, the attention of international academia has been focused upon them constantly. The districts and certain of their key players (Benetton, Del Vecchio, Della Valle, Prada,

Beretta, and Alessi, for example) are the only Italian phenomena to which prestigious international business schools devote their case studies. Beginning in the second half of the 1980s, chapters on the Italian districts have appeared in the works of scholars at the most important American universities, such as M. Porter (Harvard) and C. Sabel (M.I.T., Columbia). The capacity of the Italian districts to reconcile development and employment has even been the subject of meetings of the Group of Seven (Detroit, 1995) and of the European Union summit conference in Lille (1996). In fact, on the same physical foundation of products and postmodern organizational structures, two depictions of Italy have developed: the mercantile image of Italian style and the political

GP RT Exopower ski boot.

Design by Centro Stile Benetton.

Benetton System Nordica

(Courtesy ADI, Milan)

Meridiana. Ceiling lamp.

Design, Fabio Reggiani. Reggiani Illuminazione

(Courtesy, ADI, Milan)

and academic model, which has sought and continues to seek in Italy's industrial districts the shape of things to come for postindustrial societies.

The Entrepreneurial Style

The success and the competitive advantage of the industrial districts are sometimes attributed to traditions or to the special union and tax treatment afforded to small companies. The unusual atmosphere that one can sense in the districts has contributed in a crucial manner to the commercial performance of "Made in Italy"; that alone, however, cannot explain the causes of the prolonged international success of Italian suits, ties, eyeglasses, shoes, furniture, household furnishings, and jewelry in an open global market.

Only recently has an effort been made to shed some light on a few constant features in the behavior of entrepreneurs in the districts; the fieldwork done to date makes it possible to delineate an entrepreneurial style that may not be amazingly refined but that is certainly effective. Here, too, we see a way of working that is consistent with the particular image of Made in Italy; once again, a comparison with British and American or Japanese models is extremely informative.

In Italy, there are sixty-eight companies for every one thousand inhabitants, as compared with the forty-six in Great Britain, the thirty-seven in Germany, and the thirty-five in France. The "animal spirits" of Italian entrepreneurs are not daunted by language barriers, an inefficient public sector, or the small size of the companies. There are more than 170,000 companies that export, and in 90 percent of these companies, their foreign sales are less than two million dollars. It is a veritable army of small businessmen who, armed only with courage, suitcases, and sets of samples, travel tirelessly to the four corners of the world ("a people of poets, artists, heroes, saints, thinkers, scientists, navigators . . .").

"Minimalist" Organizational Structures and Leadership

The operation of the districts is well ahead of the fashionable approaches described in management journals and magazines in recent years; they are lightly structured with minimal staffs and their

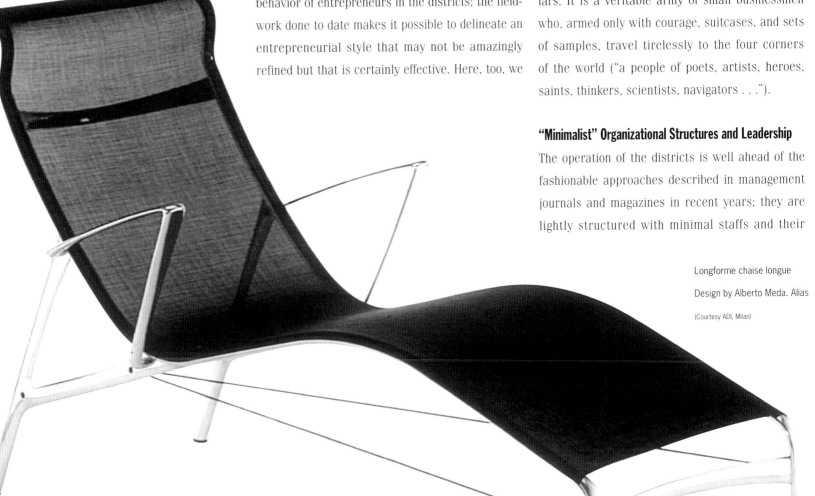

Longforme chaise longue

Design by Alberto Meda. Alias

(Courtesy ADI, Milan)

relationships are organized into networks. The chronic shortage of secretaries, executives, and managers keeps internal pressure high, and all of this cannot be explained simply as a decision to adapt to the troughs—as opposed to the crests—of business cycles; it is a tacit rule that reflects the very basic way in which the organization of labor and work is conceived, and indirect functions are structured efficiently. Even if the organizational structures are often not arranged into formal hierarchical charts, in the minds of the entrepreneurs they are sufficiently clear to allow for emergency plans and to react in a timely fashion in the face of unexpected events: a market shutdown (in recent months, for example, the financial temblors that have swept through the Asian markets) or a young and promising employee who leaves the company to work for a rival.

The companies in the districts tend to be family run; the presence of the entrepreneur can be sensed everywhere, but it is not a dominant figure. Often the entrepreneur manages to make up for his or her ubiquity by allowing broad margins of autonomy in particular functions. To borrow a phrase from another fashion in management magazines, all of this smacks of empowerment.

The entrepreneurs in the districts see each other often, and their interpersonal dynamics are quite remarkable. In particular, they are never satisfied with whatever they have achieved; they abhor stasis, and even when it would appear that all is going well, they are constantly planning to seek out new ideas, markets, products, processes, sources of supply, and forms of organization.

When consumers anywhere in the world purchase a product marked "Made in Italy," they are often consuming a depiction of Italy or, perhaps we should say, of the "Italian way of life," of the *saper vivere italiano*. The link, however, between these goods and their Italian-ness runs even deep-

Combi espresso maker and coffee grinder

Design by Richard Sapper, Alessi

(Courtesy ADI, Milan)

er. They reflect more than a way of life; they are the product of an unusual path of industrial development that takes its power from a set of institutions, a social fabric, various forms of organization, and an entrepreneurial culture that history has accumulated in Italy's industrial districts.

Zoombike folding urban bicycle

Design by Richard Sapper, Ing. Francis Ferrarin, Elettromontaggi

(Courtesy ADI, Milan)

Magò broom.

Design by Stefano Giovannoni. Magis

(Courtesy ADI, Milan)

Bootleg "extreme urban" bicycle

Design by Ufficio Tecnico Cinelli, Cinelli

(Courtesy ADI, Milan)

Rodope table lamp

Design by Zed Artemide

(Courtesy ADI, Milan)

191

Kisses from Italy, Alitalia Boeing 747 sponsored by Perugina.

Contributors

Carlo Antonelli

Carlo Antonelli is a producer for the record label Sugar and is a writer and music critic. He is the coauthor, with Fabio De Luca, of the collections of essays *Discoinferno: Storia della Dance Italiana dalla Preistoria ad Oggi* (Theoria, Rome, 1995) and *Fuori Tutti: Una Generazione in Camera Sua* (Einaudi, Turin, 1996, with photography by Marco Delogu). In 1997 and 1998, he developed and wrote (with Lilli Forina) a Raieducational television series, *Infinito Futuro*. He teaches seminars on musical aesthetics at the Istituto Europeo di Design in Milan.

Paola Antonelli

Paola Antonelli is a curator for the Department of Architecture and Design at the Museum of Modern Art in New York and a critic of architecture and design. She has worked on the editorial staffs of *Domus* (1987-91) and *Abitare* (1992-94). She taught from 1991 to 1993 at the University of California at Los Angeles. She has a degree in architecture from the Milan Politecnico.

Alberto Baccari

Alberto Baccari earned a degree in psychology at the University of Padua and studied at New York University for a postgraduate degree in film production. In 1983, he founded Baccari Associates of New York. From 1985 to 1992, he was the creative director of Armando Testa Advertising in New York, supervising advertising campaigns for clients such as E. & J. Gallo, Philip Morris, Paul Smart, Longines, Citterio, Italian Shoe Consortium, Anne Klein, Campari, Martex, Paketa, BMW, San Pellegrino, Lavazza, and De Cecco. Since 1992, he has worked in New York and Europe with leading agencies and major clients, such as Burger King, Prudential, and IBM. He has received numerous international awards and citations including the Clio, One Show, Cannes, N.Y. Art Director's Club, D&AD (British AD's Club), British Int'l TV Award, Chicago Int'l, Epica, Advertising Age's Best Award, NY Int'l, Creativity, Triennale di Milano (Industrial Design), and Communication Art Ad Award.

Andrea Balestri

Andrea Balestri, economist, has directed the Centro Studi della Unione Industriale Pratese (Prato Industrial Union Study Center) since 1988 and has also run the Communications and Promotion Unit of the same organization since 1993. He regularly lectures at universities and training centers (faculty of engineering, Florence; degree course in Prato; LIUC in Castellanza; Bocconi in Milan; Hosey University in Tokyo). He is a member of the Secretariat of the Club dei Distretti Industriali (Industrial Districts Club). He edits two periodicals (the monthly *Pratofutura* and the quarterly *Distretti Italiani*) and has published numerous articles and monographs in *Science and Experiments*, *La Laniera*, *Mondo Economico*, *La Nazione*, *Il Sole 24 Ore*, *L'Impresa*, *Sviluppo Locale*, *Economia e Management*, and *L'Illustrazione Italiana*.

Fausto Colombo

Fausto Colombo is associate professor of theory and techniques of mass communications at the Università Cattolica of Milan. He is the director of the Osservatorio sulla Comunicazione and associate director of the Scuola di Specializzazione in Analisi e Gestione della Comunicazione (School of Higher Studies in the Analysis and Management of Communications) for the same university. His academic work has been marked by an effort to direct the study of media into a multidisciplinary field that allows full use of the resources of social history and cultural sociology. Aside from the more traditional media (cinema, television, newspapers, and the so-called new media), he focuses on less commonly studied media, such as popular publishing, the stage, and opera. Among his publications are *Gli Archivi Imperfetti* (Vita e Pensiero Milan 1986), *I Persuasori non Occulti* (Lupetti, Milan 1989), *Ombre Sintetiche* (Liguori, Naples, 1990; 2nd ed., 1995), *Le Nuove Tecnologie della Comunicazione* (Bompiani, Milan, 1994, with Gianfranco Bettetini), *Dizionario della Pubblicità* (Zanichelli, Bologna, 1994, with Alberto Abruzzese); *Media e Industria Culturale* (1994), *Il Testo Visibile: Storia, Teoria e Modelli di Analisi* (NIS, Rome, 1996, with Ruggero Eugeni), *La Cultura Sottile: Media e Industria Culturale in Italia dall'Ottocento agli Anni Novanta* (Bompiani, Milan, 1998), and *Media, Eros e Civiltà* (Costa e Nolan, Milan, 1998, with Gianfranco Bettetini). He is a consultant for RAI television for the planning of educational programming.

Leslie Fratkin

Leslie Fratkin is a photographer based in New York City. She travels frequently, working for a wide range of publications in the U.S. and overseas. In 1995 she went to Bosnia and the city of Sarajevo where she met with many local photographers, filmmakers, and other artists, leading her to create *Sarajevo Self-Portrait: The View from Inside*, an exhibition and book project combining the images and the stories, in their own words, of ten photographers from the former Yugoslavia. In 1997 she received a fellowship from the Soros Foundation and a grant from the Trust for Mutual Understanding, both for the continued development and support of *Sarajevo Self-Portrait*.

Thomas Hine

Thomas Hine is a writer on design, popular culture and architecture. He is the author of *Populuxe*, an examination of the look and life of America during the 1950s and 1960s, which gave the English language a new word to describe the style of the period. He is also the author of *The Total Package* and *The Rise and Fall of the American Teenager*, to be published by Avon in September 1999.

Franco La Cecla

Franco La Cecla is a researcher at the University of Bologna; he also teaches the sociology of interethnic relations at the University of Palermo and cultural anthropology at the University of Ravenna. Among his books are *Perdersi: l'Uomo Senza Ambiente* (Bari, 1988), *Mente Locale, per un'Antropologia dell'Abitare* (Rome, 1993), *Il Malinteso: Antropologia dell'Incontro* (Bari, 1997), *Bambini per Strada* (Milan, 1995) and *Perfetti e Invisibili: l'Immagine dell'Infanzia nei Media* (Milan, 1996), the catalog of an exhibition he organized for Pitti Immagine in Florence.

David Le Boutillier

David Le Boutillier is the founder and owner of the Eidolon Consulting Group, a restaurant consulting and development firm. The firm specializes in the conceptualization, design, and development of independent restaurants. His restaurants have been recognized by *Esquire Magazine* (Best New Restaurants of 1997), the *Los Angeles Times*, *Travel and Leisure*, *Travel Holiday*, *The Wine Spectator*, and *Atlanta Magazine*.

Richard Martin

Richard Martin, curator of the Costume Institute of the Metropolitan Museum of Art, is adjunct professor of art history and archaeology at Columbia University and adjunct professor of art at New York University. From 1974 to 1988, he was editor of *Arts Magazine*, and for twenty years he taught art history at the Fashion Institute of Technology, where he also served as executive director of the Shirley Goodman Resource Center and executive director of the Educational Foundation for the Fashion Industries. His many books include *Fashion and Surrealism*, *The New Urban Landscape*, *Contemporary Fashion*, and *St. James Fashion Encyclopaedia*. His books on Charles James and Gianni Versace were published in 1977. His hundreds of essays have appeared in journals as diverse as *Artforum*, the *New York Times*, the *Los Angeles Times*, *L'Uomo Vogue*, the *International Herald Tribune*, *Journal of Design History*, *Mondo Uomo*, and *Journal of American Culture*. He is author or co-author of innumerable exhibition catalogs, including *Splash: A History of Swimwear*, *The Historical Mode: Fashion and Art in the 1980s*, *Jocks and Nerds: Men's Style in the Twentieth Century*, *Infra-Apparel*, *Orientalism*, *Haute Couture*, *Christian Dior*, and *The Four Seasons*. Among his recent honors are Pratt's "Excellence by Design" Award, Laboratory Institute of Merchandising's Distinguished Achievement Award, an honorary doctorate from Otis College of Art & Design, election as a fellow of the Costume Society of America, and a special award for "furthering fashion as art and culture" from the Council of Fashion Designers of America in 1996.

Fiona Morgan

Fiona Morgan is a freelance writer and staff member at *Salon Magazine* in San Francisco. She is a recent graduate of the creative writing and drama programs of the University of Washington in Seattle. In addition to Italy, she writes about Texas, North Carolina, and other places she has lived, and about culture and the arts.

Peppino Ortoleva

Peppino Ortoleva is the author of approximately one hundred essays and books on the history and theory of communications. Among his most recent books are *Mediastoria: Comunicazione e Mutamento Sociale nel Mondo Contemporaneo* (Parma, 1995) and *Un Ventennio a Colori: Televisione Privata e Società in Italia* (Florence, 1995). He teaches theory and techniques of new media in the communications sciences program at the University of Turin and is a partner in Cliomedia, a company that has been active for the last decade in the field of multimedia production, mass communications, and historical and social research.

Ted Polhemus

Ted Polhemus is an anthropologist who, since the 1970s, has concentrated on the relationship between youth culture and fashion. Among his many publications are *Fashion & Anti-Fashion* (1975) and *Street Style: From Sidewalk to Catwalk* (1994), which was published in conjunction with an exhibition of the same name at the Victoria & Albert Museum in London.

Marco Ricchetti

Marco Ricchetti, an economist, was born in Lecco in 1956. After receiving a postgraduate degree in economics fromthe College of Europe in Bruges, he undertook numerous studies on the fields of textiles and apparel manufacturing in Italy and Europe, focusing especially on the deregulation of international trade, the internationalization of manufacturing, the processes of restructuring in the textiles manufacturing regions of Europe, the structure of the textiles and apparel manufacturing sector in Italy, and industrial policies. He is a partner in Hermes Lab, a consultant in economic studies for the Associazioni Imprenditoriali dell'Industria Tessile, and coordinator for the research office for Federtessile.

Saskia Sassen

Saskia Sassen is a professor of sociology at the University of Chicago. Her most recent books are *Globalization and Its Discontents: Selected Essays 1984-1998* (New York, New Press, 1998) and *Losing Control? Sovereignty in an Age of Globalization* (New York, Columbia University Press, 1996). Her books have been translated into several languages. *The Global City* has recently appeared in French (Descartes, Paris, 1996), Italian (UTET, Milan, 1998), and Spanish (UBA, Buenos Aires, 1998). She is currently completing *Immigration Policy in the Global Economy: From National Crisis to Multilateral Management*, sponsored by the Twentieth Century Fund, and has begun a new project on cities and their crossborder networks sponsored by the United Nations University.

Alix Sharkey

Alix Sharkey began his journalistic career in 1981 with the ground-breaking style magazine *i-D*. He has written about nightlife, fashion, media, advertising, and youth culture for the *Guardian*, the *Independent*, the *Sunday Times*, and the *Observer*, and he was news editor of *MTV Europe* from 1992 to 1993. He contributes to various European and American publications including *Dazed & Confused*, Condé Nast *Traveller*, *Das Magazine*, and *Courrier International*, and he currently lives in London.

Antony Shugaar

Antony Shugaar is a reporter, translator, and author. He has published several books (Arcadia, Aguilar, Smithmark), translated numerous books and essays (Harvard University Press, Abbeville Press, the M.I.T. Press, and others), and published extensively as a journalist (*N.Y. Observer*, *Spy*, *New York Magazine*, *Photo District News*, *Wigwag*, *New England Monthly*, *The Lytton Times*, and others). He has been a member of the planning and production team that created *The Style Engine* and *Volare*. He has a special interest in the media business and the conveyance of meaning in pop, popular, and classical cultures.

Pierre Sorlin

Pierre Sorlin is a professor of the sociology of audiovisual media at the Sorbonne, Paris. He is the author of *Sociologia del Cinema* (Mondadori), *Il Film nella Storia* (Nuova Italia), *Estetiche degli Audiovisivi* (Nuova Italia), and the forthcoming *L'Immagine e l'Evento* (Paravia).

Valerie Steele

Valerie Steele is chief curator of the Museum at the Fashion Institute of Technology. A cultural historian, she taught for a decade in the division of graduate studies at F.I.T. She is the author of several books, including *50 Years of Fashion: New Look to Now* (Yale University Press, 1997); *Fetish: Fashion, Sex and Power* (New York, Oxford University Press, 1996); *Women of Fashion: 20th-Century Designers* (Rizzoli, 1991); *Paris Fashion: A Cultural History* (OUP, 1988), and *Fashion and Eroticism* (OUP, 1985). She is also co-editor of *Men and Women: Dressing the Part* (Smithsonian, 1989). She supervised the organization of the exhibition *Art, Design and Barbie: The Making of a Cultural Icon*, for which she wrote the catalog (Rizzoli. 1995). She has lectured widely on subjects such as *Youthquake: The Fashion of the 1960s* (Kimbell Art Museum), *Dressing for Work* (Valentine Museum), *Uniforms and Sexual Stereotypes* (American Studies Association), *The Myth of the 16-Inch Waist* (American Historical Association), *The Italian Look* (Fordham University), *Fashion and Fragrance* (Chicago Historical Society), *Erotic Fashion Photography* (Seminar on the History of Psychiatry and Behavioural Sciences, The New York Hospital—Cornell Medical Center), *Fashion, Sex and Power* (Association of Women in Apparel Resources), and *Women in Fashion* (World Congress of Sociology, Madrid). Editor of the new quarterly journal *Fashion Theory: The Journal of Dress, Body & Culture* (Berg Publishers), she has also contributed essays to many other periodicals ranging from *Aperture* and *Artforum* to *Visionnaire* and *Vogue*. She has served on the board of directors of the Costume Society of America and the advisory board of the International Costume Association (based in Tokyo), and she is a member of the Fashion Group International.

Kaoru Tashiro

Kaoru Tashiro, born in Tokyo, is a freelance journalist and editorial coordinator for Japanese magazines. She writes about Italian creativity, focusing upon "i-shoku-ju," or "clothing, eating, and living" as a unified art. She contributes to various magazines, including *Brutus*, *Marie Claire Japon*, *Trendsetter*, *Fashion Hanbai*, and *The Card*. She has worked in Milan since 1990.

Carlo Tombola

Carlo Tombola is a freelance author and geographer who lives and teaches in Milan. He is the author (with R. Mainardi) of *Grandi Città ed Aree Metropolitane* (Milan, 1982) and (with S. Finardi) *Il Sistema Mondiale dei Trasporti* (Bologna, 1995). He is also the author of numerous articles in newspapers and magazines on the transformations of the territory of Italy.

Ugo Volli

Ugo Volli teaches the philosophy of language at the University of Bologna and semiotics at the Università IULM of Milan. He works on problems of communications in both practical and theoretical terms. He has worked for many years on the study of fashion, publishing, among other things, *Contro la Moda* (Feltrinelli, 1988), *Una Scrittura del Corpo* (Stampa Alternativa, 1998), *Block Modes* (Lupetti, 1998). He also writes for *La Repubblica*, *Il Mattino*, *Grazia*, and *Liberal*. Among the most recent of his several books are *Il Libro della Comunicazione* (Il Saggiatore, 1994), *Come Leggere il Telegiornale* (Laterza, 1995), *Fascino* (Feltrinelli, 1997), and *Il Televoto* (Franco Angeli, 1997).

We would like to thank the individuals and organizations
listed here for their kind assistance:

Carlo Bertelli
Giovanna Bertelli
Stefano Giovannoni
Lisa Lytton
Antonio Maffeis
Stefano Pandini
Carla Pozzi
Kazuhiro Saito
Hijiri Sakisaka
Kristin Schelter
Ferdinando Scianna
Alfredo Stola

ADI—Associazione per il Disegno Industriale, Milan
Civica Raccolta delle Stampe A. Bertarelli, Milan
Fondazione Cineteca Italiana, Milan
Insignia/ESG, New York City
Italian Trade Commission, New York City
Neue Pinakothek, Munich
Touring Club Italiano—Archivi Alinari, Milan

Armando Testa Spa, Turin
Bates Italia Spa, Milan
BGS DMB&B Srl, Milan
BRW & Partners Srl, Milan
McCann-Erickson, London
McCann-Erickson Paris
Ogilvy & Mather Spa, Milan
Studio Immagine Srl, Milan

Art Show
Brutus
Der Spiegel
Esquire, Japan
GQ—Gentleman's Quarterly, Germany
Holiday
Max
National Geographic Magazine
Rassegna
Salon On-Line Magazine
Vogue—Condé Nast, U.S.A.

Alitalia Spa
Aprilia Spa
Boeing U.S.A.
Buitoni Spa
Bulgari Spa
Cagiva Motor Spa
Dean & Deluca U.S.A.
Dolce & Gabbana Spa
Ducati Motor Spa
Ermenegildo Zegna Spa
Ferrari Spa

Gianfranco Ferrè Spa
Gianni Versace Spa
Giorgio Armani Spa
Gruppo Editoriale Sugarmusic Srl
Gruppo Stola Spa
Gucci Spa
Illycaffé Spa
Lavazza Spa
Martini & Rossi Spa
Moschino MoonShadow Spa
National Geographic Society
Prada — I.P.I. Services Spa
Seat Spa

Arte: "Metropolis," Reiner Penzhol
BBC 2: "Antonio Carluccio's Show," Bazal Productions
Ceska Televize: "Jedna rodina," Kamila Kytkova
CFMT Channel 47: "Noi Oggi"
Channel 1, Televisione Nazionale Bulgara
Channel 4: "Gazzetta Football Italia"
Channel 4: "Euroballs '98," Rapido Tv
CNN: "Style"
Conquest Network, Luca Lindner
CTN, Chinese Television Network: "Fashion on Air," Rita Kao
CTN, Chinese Television Network: "Melodia," Media
Food Network: "Molto Mario"Fashion News
Infas Tv Tokyo: "Fashion Tsushin," Emilia Watanabe
KBS, Korean Broadcasting System
MBC, Munhwa Broadcasting Corporation
MTV: "Stylissimo"
National Italian American Foundation, Dianne Gale
Orbit, Arabic Channels: "Motor," "Anaqa," Khulub Abu Homos
RCTI, Rajawali Citra Television Indonesia, Adolf Posuma
RTE 1, Radio Telefís Éireann: "Italianissimo"
RTL 4: "It's Fantastic Here," Joop van den Ende Tv-
Producties bv
SABC, South African Broadcasting Corporation
Slovenia Tv: "Trend," Jozica Brodaric
TSI, Televisione Svizzera Italiana: "Vicini in Europa," Tito
Malaguerra
TV 2 Danmark: "Pasta Plus," Feline Munck
TV 3: "Uno x Due," Thomas Nordhal

VOLARE